# YOU WERE MADE FOR LOVE

## W9-ALK-152

In this engaging and inspiring book Philip Carlson points us to the ultimate love affair—the relationship that frail human beings can have with the God who chooses to embrace us in spite of our waywardness. Carlson effectively draws on the struggles of his own life and ministry in providing counsel for our own journeys. This is a book that deserves a wide Christian audience!

RICHARD J. MOUW
PRESIDENT AND PROFESSOR OF CHRISTIAN PHILOSOPHY,
FULLER SEMINARY

You are the one that Jesus loves. Philip Carlson will help you not just know it but feel it.

JOHN ORTBERG
AUTHOR AND PASTOR

In *You Were Made For Love*, Philip Carlson reveals a biblical pathway to personal growth and lasting impact. With eloquent simplicity, he guides us into a deepening experience of God's love and takes us on a journey of expressing this life-changing love to a hurting world.

DEAN CARLSON, D.MIN.
OC INTERNATIONAL AFRICA AREA DIRECTOR

Philip Carlson has poured his heart into this book, and as a result, the pages overflow with genuine love. Rather than simply expounding on important concepts, he invites the reader to join him in a personal conversation. Drawing deeply from Scripture and an engaging mix of vivid illustrations and moving stories from his own life, he convincingly conveys that "true love" is no empty platitude or unobtainable ideal but rather a vibrant reality well within reach.

JEFF BJORCK, PH.D.
LICENSED CLINICAL PSYCHOLOGIST AND PROFESSOR OF
PSYCHOLOGY, FULLER THEOLOGICAL SEMINARY

You will be surprised how quickly this book reads you.

Ginny Carter
Member, Bethany Church, Sierra Madre, CA

This book is nothing less than an extravagant invitation to explore and discover love at its best, at its origins, which is the very heart of God!

Dave Jordan-Irwin
Pastor, Healdsburg Community Church,
San Francisco, CA

If you are longing for a life of greater significance, happiness, and love, read this remarkable book. Its power to change lives comes not only from the fresh perspective on biblical truths, but also from the vulnerability with which this pastor and physician shares his own journey from pain and brokenness into a life transformed by love. Dr. Carlson's words and life persuasively beckon us to risk living the ultimate adventure of loving and being loved.

KEVIN AND KAY MARIE BRENNFLECK
AUTHORS, *LIVE YOUR CALLING: A PRACTICAL GUIDE TO FINDING AND FULFILLING YOUR MISSION IN LIFE*

# YOU WERE MADE for LOVE

### EMBRACING THE LIFE
### YOU WERE MEANT TO LIVE

## PHILIP CARLSON

LIFE JOURNEY®

*Bringing Home the Message for Life*

COOK COMMUNICATIONS MINISTRIES
Colorado Springs, Colorado • Paris, Ontario
KINGSWAY COMMUNICATIONS LTD
Eastbourne, England

Life Journey® is an imprint of
Cook Communications Ministries, Colorado Springs, CO 80918
Cook Communications, Paris, Ontario
Kingsway Communications, Eastbourne, England

YOU WERE MADE FOR LOVE
© 2006 Philip Carlson

Cover photo: Elena Ray, Shutterstock, Inc.
Cover Design: Zoë Tennesen-Eck Design

Printed in the United States of America

All Scripture, unless otherwise noted, are taken from the *Holy Bible,
Today's New International Version*®. Copyright © 2001, 2005 by
International Bible Society. Used by permission of Zondervan. All
rights reserved. Scripture quotations marked PH are taken from J. B.
Phillips: The New Testament in Modern English, revised editions ©
J. B. Phillips, 1958, 1960, 1972, permission of Macmillan Publishing
Co. and Collins Publishers. Italics in Scripture have been added by
the author for emphasis.

ISBN-13 978-0-7394-8406-7

To John Glandon, Robert Schaper,
Robert VanderZaag, Brice Carlson,
Merton Alexander, Sky Aijian,
Bill Ashe, Al Elby,
Graham Patterson, Jim McReynolds,
Mel Friesen, Paul Byer,
Colin Brown, Jim Bradley,
Richard Foster, and David Gatewood—

*men who made God's love real to my heart
and set my feet firmly on the path to following Jesus*

# Contents

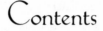

## Part Three: How Does Love Grow?
### Isaiah 58:1–12

# Acknowledgments

Heartfelt love and gratitude to the men whose names are listed in the dedication of this book—my great-grandfather John Glandon, my childhood pastors and mentors Bob Schaper and Robert VanderZaag, mentors and spiritual fathers Brice Carlson, Merton Alexander, Sky Aijian, Bill Ashe, Al Elby, Graham Patterson, Jim McReynolds, Mel Friesen, Paul Byer, Colin Brown, Jim Bradley, Richard Foster, and David Gatewood. Their role in loving, guiding, and directing has helped shape my life and the content of this book.

Carole, whose love has made my life fuller than I ever imagined possible—the last eighteen years have "seemed like only a few days ..."—along with

Jonathan, Caitlin, Brendan, and Ciara—have all offered their love, encouragement, and support throughout the course of writing this book. How can I thank you enough? We are grateful to our parents and family for their love and support and for their willingness to allow me to share some uncomfortable seasons in our lives in order to make clear the power of God's love. We love you all.

Thanks to Kevin and Kay Marie Brennfleck, Florence Littauer, and Jan Coleman for your help and encouragement in getting me to write a proposal and move forward. I am grateful to Beth Woodin for volunteering her help in aspects of preparing the manuscript. Jeff and Sharon Bjorck, Don and Anita Lewis, Jack and Ginny Carter, Amy Varin, Lois Mintz, Debby Grant, and Terri Owens all invested hours in reading the manuscript and offering valuable criticism and insight. Thank you.

Mike Nappa has been far more than a gifted editor. The joy and enthusiasm with which he embraced this project from the moment it came across his desk, as well as his warm, gentle spirit, have been a constant source of encouragement and inspiration. His insightful feedback and direction have been beyond value. Thank you, Mike. Special thanks to the whole team at Cook Communications Ministries for their hard work, including Diane Gardner, Mike Warden, Susan Miller, and everyone else who contributed along the way.

Thank you to the whole family at Bethany Church, where we are learning together to allow God's love to flow through our lives. The love we share is a precious gift.

I always thought love was important. I had no idea how wonderful and important it was until I met Jesus. Apart from his life and death none of us would ever really understand what love is.

Thank you for taking time to read this book. I hope some things here might help you open your heart to God's love and understand how much you matter to him.

Philip Carlson
Sierra Madre, California

# Introduction

Some of my best thinking and praying and jousting with personal demons happens during late-night walks or sitting alone in the darkness after everyone else has gone to bed. I've never been a great sleeper. Part of the problem is that I've always viewed sleep as a necessary interruption to things I would rather be doing.

It seems that men in their forties spend a lot of time thinking about life, especially at night. Several years ago, on a dark, quiet winter night alone in the living room I had a moment of exquisite clarity in which I realized that my life was not turning out the way it should have. All the indicators in my early life pointed to the likelihood of failure and disaster. A wounding relationship with an alcoholic father had produced a deep brokenness in me, and my own foolish choices had compounded the damage. But here I sat in a home filled with peace, where everyone loved each other, where I knew I was loved, experiencing a quietness and peace I had never known in the first half of my life.

I was so struck by this realization that in the days that followed I began a painstaking and honest exploration to understand what had happened in my life to account for such a miraculous change of outcome.

Don't get me wrong. Not everything in my life is as it should be. I continue to sense how resistant my heart can be to change and growth. I still struggle against doing the very things I don't want to do. I am often driven by the by-products of my brokenness—the need to be special, to stand out, to prove myself worthwhile. The list goes on.

But somewhere along the way, something essential in me had changed. As I look back over the years I have come to the conclusion that the transformation of my heart—however unfinished it may still be—can only be explained by the impact of love upon my life. The love of others—given freely and tenaciously—slowly freed me to lower my defenses and consider the possibility that God also loved me. When I finally did connect with God's love, it was a lot bigger and more amazing than anything I had ever imagined possible. In the grip of his love I experienced a freedom in which I was actually able to see beyond my own needs and discover a whole new world of opportunities and dreams.

You and I were made for love. God created us with a deep need to be loved as well as a tremendous capacity to give love. We function best, live most happily, experience the greatest satisfaction when we know we are loved. Why is it, then, that so few of us ever do?

I believe that the deepest longing of the human soul is a hunger for God and a need to experience the love that only he can give. It seems to me that the two most significant obstructions to the healing and transformation of the heart are the failure to understand, receive, and live in the flow of God's unconditional love, and the inability to pour that same love into the lives of others.

Jesus expressed two foundational concerns repeatedly—one had to do with the condition of our hearts (Mark 7:1–23; Matt. 15:1–20) and the other with our capacity for love (Matt. 22:36–40). Tested in his theology by an expert in the Law, Jesus was asked to name the greatest commandment in the Law. "Jesus replied: 'Love the Lord your God with all your heart and with all your soul and with all your mind.' This is the first and greatest commandment. And the second is like it: 'Love your neighbor as yourself.' All the Law and the Prophets hang on these two commandments" (Matt. 22:37–40).

What about us? Do we love God in this all-consuming way? Do we love ourselves appropriately in light of our experience of his love? Do we love others deeply, compassionately, sacrificially? Jesus' concern for all of us is that we be freed to love deeply from a transformed heart.

Our capacity for love—both giving and receiving—reflects the condition of our hearts.

We hear a lot about love and grace in religious circles and may even have a well-developed theology of love. But something seems to keep the power of this message from penetrating our hearts. Until God's love penetrates, permeates, and captivates our hearts we are at risk for an anemic, passionless spirituality.

Sometimes at night when I cannot sleep, I look in on my children. Often this nighttime vigil turns to prayer, and sometimes my prayers turn into dreams for their well-being. These are not the kind of dreams that would lead me to pressure or manipulate my children, but the kind of dreams born of hope and care—hope that they will escape some of my pain and brokenness, avoid some of my failings, hope that they will become good people, live wisely, and walk closely with Jesus. Our Father has such dreams for us. He longs for our best. His highest hope is that our hearts would be set free, that we would allow him to love us, learn to love more deeply, and give ourselves fully to the things that matter most to him. Imagine a life lived from a heart renovated by the grace of God!

This is a book for those hungering for meaningful, fulfilling relationships. I believe that we can grow in our capacity for love. We can become more radically inclusive. We can be freed from self-service and self-absorption. But this transformation requires us to follow Jesus into a life of radical, world-changing love and service.

The growth of love is a process, but one with clearly defined and necessary steps. I've organized these steps around three basic questions: Where does love come from? What does love look like? How does love grow? Answering each of these questions carefully and truthfully is crucial to learning how to allow ourselves to be possessed by God's kind of love and to giving that same love away to others. The purpose of this book is to explore the strategy by which God makes us into more loving people. Let's see if we can dig down and make plain and practical the key ideas regarding the growth of love in a human heart and make sense of them in the places where we work and live. This process will not look exactly the same for everyone, but when the underlying steps are understood and practiced, they will lead us all to a place where love is continually growing. The growth of love is a breathtaking adventure, because it is on this road more than any other that we will meet Jesus.

*Part One*

❧

# Where Does Love Come From?

Dear friends, let us love one another, for love comes from God. Everyone who loves has been born of God and knows God. Whoever does not love does not know God, because God is love. This is how God showed his love among us: He sent his one and only Son into the world that we might live through him. This is love: not that we loved God, but that he loved us and sent his Son as an atoning sacrifice for our sins. Dear friends, since God so loved us, we also ought to love one another. No one has ever seen God; but if we love one another, God lives in us and his love is made complete in us.

This is how we know that we live in him and he in us: He has given us of his Spirit. And we have seen and testify that the Father has sent his Son to be the Savior of the world. If anyone acknowledges that Jesus is the Son of God, God lives in them and they in God. And so we know and rely on the love God has for us.

God is love. Whoever lives in love lives in God, and God in them. This is how love is made complete among us so that we will have confidence on the day of judgment: In this world we are like Jesus. There is no fear in love. But perfect love drives out fear, because fear has to do with punishment. The one who fears is not made perfect in love.

We love because he first loved us. If we say we love God yet hate a brother or sister, we are liars. For if we do not love a fellow believer, whom we have seen, we cannot love God, whom we have not seen. And he has given us this command: Those who love God must also love one another.

—1 John 4:7–21

# 1

# The Transforming Power
# of Being Loved:
# Significance

W e were walking through a crowded night market in the town where I grew up. The crisp spring evening was tainted only by the sense of dullness I felt, having been on call in the hospital as a resident for the previous forty hours. Carole was walking up ahead of me with our two older children hanging on her. I was in charge of keeping track of Brendan, who had recently turned two and was experiencing the joy of exercising a small measure of independence. He wandered off in different directions, but every twenty to thirty seconds looked back to check in and make sure he could still see me. I saw it as an opportunity to study his reactions to the world and I hung back a little, never taking my eyes off him. Suddenly his expression changed. He was looking for me but couldn't see me, and a look of dread spread across his face. His pain and fear were obvious. Not wanting to prolong his anguish I raised my arms and waved them. He spotted me immediately. His concern quickly melted away. He wandered off.

It occurred to me that if you were to ask two-year-old Brendan what had happened it would have been clear to him that he found me. But the truth of the matter was that I was there all the time, never taking my eyes off of him, caring for him and protecting him.

This is what happens in our experience of God. From our perspective, we seek and find him. We read, we search, we listen, we pray, we discover. It's our initiative. We often hear people claiming to find God. In reality God was there all the time, loving us, refusing to give up on us, persistent in his pursuit of us.

Pascal's description of a God-shaped vacuum in the human heart describes a crucial dimension of our humanity. The God-shaped vacuum in the human spirit is a love-shaped vacuum. Ripping God from the human experience, as our culture has attempted to do, leaves the human spirit with a sense of aloneness and need that nothing can fill. A. W. Tozer captures the human dilemma:

> We are lonely with an ancient and cosmic loneliness. We are each like a little child lost in a crowded market, who has strayed but a few feet from its mother, yet because she cannot be seen, the child is inconsolable. So we try by every method devised by religion to relieve our fears and heal our hidden sadness; but with all our efforts we remain

unhappy still, with the settled despair of men alone in a vast and deserted universe.[1]

But God is constantly looking for us, pursuing us, and it is he who chooses us (Eph. 1:4, 11; John 15:16). Before we ever thought of God, he thought of us. Before we loved him, he loved us. Before any winsome or redemptive act on our part, he set a plan into motion at great expense to himself to save us. We are loved even before we begin to exist. Before we were conceived God already knew us and loved us and wrote a multivolume work about each of our lives. Before we existed as a single cell we had a history with God in which we already mattered to him (Ps. 139:13–18; Jer. 1:4–5).

# Our Drive for Significance

The question we want answered more than any other is the question of our significance. It takes many forms: Do I matter? Does my life count for something? Does anyone really care about me? Am I significant? Years spent talking with people about the problems of life have convinced me that the pain at the core of the human spirit is rooted in our inability to find satisfying answers to these most basic questions. So many people I have encountered face an overwhelming sense of insignificance, struggling to believe that their lives count for something. We are built for significance. We are driven to seek it as our bodies seek oxygen. Easy formulas and pat answers won't do. The stakes are too high. The need is too deep.

Growing up with a violent alcoholic father had many damaging effects on my soul. My hopes and dreams were often crushed. The pain of my emotional wounds was constant. I found it impossible to believe that I would ever be acceptable or lovable to anyone. I was dreadfully afraid of men from my father's generation because I was sure that if they knew me they would reject me. I felt the need to pretend I was someone else, hoping to project an image that someone might find acceptable. I learned early in life that in some situations it was easier to lie than to face the consequences that came with the truth. And in the back of my mind, I suspected that God, too, would find it hard to love me as I really was. I was very broken in many ways.

In my teen years I lived with the sense of invincibility that often comes with youth. I believed that I had escaped the horrors of abuse unscathed. I chose to ignore the past—not to forget it, not to forgive; simply to ignore. As in most dysfunctional family situations, the reality was shrouded in secrecy. An unspoken rule dictated that one must never speak of certain things. This suited me just fine. I would have been terrified and ashamed if anyone knew the truth about aspects of my earlier life.

As I look back, I have discovered that for much of my life, even as a follower of Jesus, I have been driven by the by-products of my brokenness: the self-protection that puts up a false front, keeping others from seeing who I really am; the need to prove myself worthwhile by endless hours of work "for God" that robbed me of the joy of simply being with God; and the outward deception I used to convince others that I was lovable and worthy of acceptance.

My inability to face my brokenness meant that even while walking with Jesus, I failed to understand the reality of his acceptance of me just as I am. While speaking of God's grace to others, I succumbed to the power of my compulsions by my heart-level rejection of that same grace. I often allowed the character Brennan Manning calls "the impostor" to show up and do his song and dance, not allowing myself to believe that God loved me as I really was.[2]

It was not until my early twenties, when my deep brokenness began to damage relationships with people I cared about, that I realized the harm to my soul had been severe. The damage of the abuse was compounded by my own sin and selfishness, and I came to a place where I felt a million miles away from God. I felt very little from him. I felt very little for him. I could no longer ignore what was going on inside.

When we strip away our self-protection and pretense, what is left? What is there, at the core of our being, that drives us? We are all driven by a compelling need to feel we are significant. Ernest Becker is one of my favorite writers because of his probing insight into human nature. He wrote that in childhood we make little effort to hide our struggle for self-esteem. We are unashamed about our needs and wants. Becker explains:

> The child cannot allow himself to be second-best or devalued, much less left out. "You gave him the biggest piece of candy!" "You gave him more juice!" "Here's a little more, then." "Now *she's* got more juice than me!" "You let her light the fireplace and not me." "Okay, you light a piece of paper." "But this piece of paper is *smaller* than the one she lit." And so on and on ... Sibling rivalry is a critical problem that reflects the basic human condition: it is not that children are vicious, selfish, or domineering. It is that they so openly express man's tragic destiny: he must desperately justify himself as an object of primary value in the universe.[3]

Becker also writes that in the face of death, "it is the meaning of the thing that is of paramount importance; what man really fears is not so much extinction, but extinction *with insignificance*."[4] At the age of fifty-one, after writing *War and Peace* and *Anna Karenina*, Tolstoy came to believe he had accomplished nothing in his life. As he struggled with this anxiety about the meaning of his life, he lamented in his *Confession*: "What will come of what I do today and tomorrow? What will come of my entire life? Expressed differently, the question may be: Why should I live? Why should I wish for anything or do anything? Or to put it still differently: Is there any meaning in my life that will not be destroyed by my inevitably approaching death?"[5] We all long for significance. We desire to make a difference. We want to stand out as important.

# The Great Deception

In our culture our sense of significance is usually a composite of several elements—our performance, our feelings about ourselves, and our perception of what other people think about us. Being attractive and productive and having lots of things are the main flags for attention. This cultural and emotional milieu leaves most of us worrying that we don't quite measure up. We all experience the deep pain of feeling unacceptable at times, that we don't fit in. We may feel that we are unsuccessful in the eyes of family members. We search constantly for a sense of worth and value, usually focusing on the opinions of others. We may lack the sensation of being approved of, accepted, or successful. These things leave us with an empty, aching heart as well as a sense of isolation.

Churches can be characterized by the same culture of competition and comparison experienced elsewhere. For many people the church is the last place they feel they can be themselves. The tendency to compare or compete prompts us to put on our "church self" for a few hours each Sunday. As a result, at times we may experience the church as a place filled with the ranks of the perfect and problem-free. In such an environment, it's no wonder that authenticity does not seem to be a real option.

Our failure to believe that we are important drives us ever deeper into the compulsion to work harder to prove ourselves. Absorbed by our quest for approval, it becomes increasingly difficult to stop and genuinely consider the needs of others—even though our schedules may be filled with outwardly "selfless" acts designed to make us look good. People who feel compelled to prove themselves lovable have an impaired capacity to give and receive love.

# The Truth about Us

We are complex beings with many capacities—physical, mental, psychological, emotional, and spiritual. We were created by God, in the image of God, for relationship with God, to reflect the glory of God. Our problem is not that we feel the need for significance or even that we pursue it, but that we pursue it in all the wrong places. Rather than turn to God, pursue God, or trust in him, we stubbornly try to find our way without him. In our fallen state we desperately search for some substitute for God, for something that will take away the gnawing emptiness and make us feel whole. We pursue it in a lot of bizarre places, but nothing can be found. Our pursuit of significance is a longing and a hunger for God himself. In fact, our hunger for significance is a "simple extension of the creative impulse of God," according to Dallas Willard.[6] But in our broken condition we don't recognize the nature of our need. We cannot see that only he can show us the road home. Only he can tell us who we are.

Our worth is determined by one thing—the worth God places on our lives. That worth must be tremendous if Jesus was willing to lay down his life for us. This is one of the most liberating facts I have ever come across. The implications are vast. If God loves us, and if his estimation of our value is all that matters, we are truly free. We can stop our pursuit of significance in anything else.

We need to learn God's opinion of us and trust what he says.

Paul's prayer for the Ephesians in chapter three is a heartfelt plea that they would comprehend the magnitude of the love of God for them, its incomparable vastness. To catch even a glimpse of the amazing love God feels for us would in itself be a life-altering experience.

Anne Morrow Lindbergh was painfully shy and retiring and, like her husband, Charles, did not like living in the public eye. Together they faced many tragedies. Reflecting on the impact of her marriage, she offers this clue to her great success as a writer, expressing the power of knowing that we are loved.

> To be deeply in love is, of course, a great and liberating force and the most common experience that frees ... Ideally, both members of a couple in love free each other to new and different worlds. I was no exception to the general rule. The sheer fact of finding myself loved was unbelievable and changed my world, my feelings about life and myself. I was given confidence, strength, and almost a new character. The man I was to marry believed in me and what I could do, and consequently I found I could do more than I realized.[7]

We need to be loved. We need to experience the liberating effects of the unconditional and unfailing love that only God can give us.

# An Experience of God's Love

By the time I was nine years old there was a tremendous amount of brokenness in my life. I felt great doubt about my worth. At the age of nine I met Jesus Christ at a vacation Bible school. The pastor of the church came to our fourth grade class and told about his own choice to follow Jesus as a nine-year-old, and I sensed it was a choice I needed to make. I couldn't be neutral on a matter like this. However, when the pastor made it clear that following Jesus meant giving him control of our lives, this caused some hesitation. I already felt my life to be hopelessly out of control.

As I struggled with the decision, my mood sank. I felt no peace. I slept poorly that night. The next day I climbed the steps to the pastor's office. I explained my dilemma. With great patience he described the character of Jesus—that though he is God, because of his humility and gentleness he set aside the adoration and privileges of heaven to come to take care of broken, sinful people. He died for us to make forgiveness a possibility and to restore our relationship with our heavenly Father.

I am a poor Calvinist at best, but at that moment Jesus seemed irresistible to me. I needed what he was offering—his grace, the forgiveness, the knowledge that I am loved. Pastor Schaper pulled two chairs together, and we knelt there as he led me in a prayer inviting Jesus to take up residence in my heart and to be my Lord and Savior. I wasn't sure what it all meant. Not that much changed at first. But I knew my life was taking a different direction.

A year later, on the last day of fifth grade, I had to say good-bye to my two best friends—Toni and Bill. Toni was moving to Hawaii because her father was a major in the army and had been transferred, and Bill was moving back to Michigan. I remember standing out on the street in front of Mayflower School in Monrovia and saying good-bye to Toni as she walked off toward the west on Court Street, and then to Bill as he headed south down Mayflower Avenue. I stood there watching until they were both out of sight. The persistent marine layer we call "June gloom" in California pervaded the early afternoon sky, and the gray and melancholy seeped into my soul. My sense of worth had been so attached to their friendship that it was an excruciating moment of pain, anguish, and loss, realizing that I would probably never see either of them again.

I turned back toward home and was soon halfway across the campus, in the middle of an asphalt playground, all by myself, not a soul around. Suddenly, I was stopped dead in my tracks by an abrupt sense of needing to be still. There, God spoke to me, not audibly but clearly. "Phil, I am your Father. I am your best friend. I'm not going anywhere. I will never leave you,

and I will always love you more than you can understand right now. You can't imagine how much love I
have for you. I think of you constantly. I never take my
eyes off you. I'm here for you right now." His love filled
me. It had the effect of lifting a tremendous sadness
and heaviness from my heart. It was but a minute or
two of realization about the stability and faithfulness of
God's love, a glimpse of the fatherhood of God—but it
was enough. At that moment, God began to redefine
my reason for being.

I had not realized until that moment just how good
the good news was. I had chosen to follow Jesus eleven
months earlier. I understood something of his sacrificial death for me and the resulting forgiveness of my
sin. I believed that I was bound for heaven someday.
But it was not until that moment that I grasped the
welcome home into the arms of my Father that Jesus
had made possible.

Nothing else can cure our souls of our drivenness and
compulsion to prove ourselves. Only a clear understanding of the Father's love revealed in Jesus Christ can allow
us to live as called people, free and centered in God.

That was a crucial and defining moment in my spiritual journey, because this sense of God's love has
deepened every day since. Any healing, any goodness,
any virtue that has come to my life has come through
the door God opened that day.

When people ask me why I am a Christian, several
reasons always come to mind. The first is the incredible
story of God's heart revealed in the Bible—pointing

again and again to how he pursues us with such purpose and persistence. I am also amazed by the fit between the provision made possible by Jesus and our deepest human need. All human beings share ultimate needs, longings, and aspirations that only Jesus can fulfill. I am fully convinced of that.

But beyond that, my thoughts turn to the insight into the fatherhood of God that was born in my heart that day on the playground. The Christian life is a process of opening our hearts to the love of God and letting him love us, letting him tell us what we are worth to him. One of the most joyful experiences in life occurs the moment we realize that our worth is measured not by our performance, but by what Jesus did for us on the cross. Jesus Christ is the measure of the worth and value God places upon our lives.

## —Making Love Real—

Brennan Manning, speaking of the disciple John who may have been Jesus' closest friend, reminds us that John is identified in the Gospels as "the one Jesus loved." Manning said, "If John were to be asked, 'What is your primary identity in life?' he would not reply, 'I am a disciple, an apostle, an evangelist, an author of one of the four Gospels,' but rather, 'I am the one Jesus loves.'"[8]

Good news! You can honestly, accurately accept this fact as the foundation of your identity—"I am the one Jesus loves."

Take a 3x5 card or sheet of paper and make a sign that reads, "I am the one Jesus loves." Tape it to your mirror, chest of drawers, dashboard, or some other place where you'll see it several times a day. Each time you see it, say those words aloud several times: "I am the one Jesus loves."

It is the truth!

# 2

# The Depth of Human Need:
# Objectivity

We come into this world a bundle of need. Not much changes as we grow older. At first our needs are very basic—a good feeding, a clean diaper, a comforting embrace. From the moment of our birth we demonstrate an amazing ability to cry out whenever we feel our need. With time we may learn to suppress our heart's cry. We may become skilled in our denial. Our defenses become more sophisticated. We learn awkward patterns of relationship designed to keep other people from stepping on our places of pain and need. But the reality of our need remains unchanged. As C. S. Lewis wrote, "Our whole being by its very nature is one vast need."[1]

Much of the time I live without a sense of the

extent of my need. I lack insight into my real condition. Once in a while something happens that reminds me that my sense of control over much of life is an illusion, and I am forced to reevaluate the situation. We all have moments where we deeply feel our need, recognize our limits, and long for something more. We have a sense that there is something holding us back, something vague and poorly understood that is keeping us from being all that we were meant to be.

We're all looking for that something more. Every morning thousands of bleary-eyed people within a few miles of our homes start their coffeemakers and wander out the door in search of the paper, but before they are fully awake they sense a familiar emptiness, something calling from deep inside needing to be filled. The successes for which we've worked so hard have failed to satisfy. The acquisitions that were supposed to dazzle have proven meaningless. Sometimes the nights are sleepless, filled with confusion over our lack of happiness and fulfillment. We attempt to fill the void, and some of our best efforts provide momentary relief. But our jobs cannot stand up to the psychic burden of the expectation of satisfaction placed upon them. Our marriages fail under the strain of asking more of them than they were ever intended to provide. Materialism is not congruent with our deepest human need. Our long-anticipated experiences fall flat. All of our failed attempts at happiness cause us to move step-by-step toward hopelessness and despair if we fail to understand the nature of our need.

# Understanding the Human Dilemma

Something is broken in us, something significant—not an accessory, but something essential to our humanity. Medicine provides a helpful analogy.

In medicine one skill is more critical than the ability to prescribe treatment—the ability to diagnose. Without proper diagnosis the treatment prescribed may injure the patient and the real illness may go untreated.

Carole and I discovered this long before I went to medical school. When our daughter, Caitlin, was born we were immediately struck by her beauty and awed by a sense of privilege that God would entrust her to our care. Within minutes, however, our bliss was shattered by a sense that something was terribly wrong. I asked the nurse why her chest kept heaving. The nurse said that she appeared to be struggling to breathe and made a quick call. Moments later a doctor ran into the room, took one look at her, grabbed her up in a blanket and hurried out of the room.

The first month of Caitlin's life was spent in intensive care. We learned that she had a rare anomaly that affected her airway along with other complications. Because her condition was so rare, not much was known about it by the staff of the hospital where she was born. We were told a lot of frightening things—much of which eventually proved to be misinformation.

When she was six weeks old we took her to Childrens Hospital Los Angeles where we met with Dr. Susan Downey. Dr. Downey not only understood her condition but had treated many other children with the same problem. She matter-of-factly described a course of treatment and assured us that by the time Caitlin started kindergarten all aspects of the condition would be completely resolved. As we left the hospital, it was as if a million pounds had been lifted from our shoulders. We had finally talked to someone who clearly understood her condition. The truth was life-giving.

Jesus recognized the importance of diagnosis. His view of the human condition was the main issue putting him at odds with the religious leaders of his day. He knew that the human problem extends to the core of our humanity, that it is something with roots reaching deep down into our hearts (Mark 7:1–23). It could not be addressed by rearranging the externals, changing appearances, and small bursts of "good" behavior.

If we don't know what our problem is, we will not recognize the answer even if it's right in front of us. Many people I've talked with who are not followers of Jesus indicate that their lack of interest in Jesus has nothing at all to do with what they know about Jesus or their feelings about Jesus. They simply don't see their need for Jesus or the church or the Christian message.

Many movements within psychology seek to mend what is broken in us and fail because of an inadequate understanding of the human condition. The self-absorbed perspective promoted in some aspects of psychology and self-help can make it difficult to move toward love which inevitably involves sacrifice, service, and extending ourselves meaningfully into the lives of others—all of which are aspects of emotional health and maturity. If our problem were simply a matter of the mind, then thinking differently, more positively, might provide an answer. But the problem is much bigger, the questions more complex.

Who am I? Where did I come from? How am I to live? What is the purpose and meaning of my life? What will happen to me when I die? Why do I do what I do? How do I decide what I will care about and invest my life in? When I get right down to the core, what is it that drives and motivates me to do the things I do? How aware am I of what I am doing and why I am doing it?

These essential questions have had many possible answers over the centuries. One measure of the validity of the answers is how they address our deepest needs. Truth is by its nature liberating and life-giving. It provides an accurate map for making choices about how to live. What good are our philosophies if they do not squarely address what's really going on inside of us? One of the most compelling arguments for the truthfulness of Jesus' teaching is the way it corresponds with gritty reality, the way it so perfectly fits like hand in glove with our deepest human need. There is an amazing coherence in his answers to these crucial questions. Because he knows who we are, Jesus consistently leads us to ultimate reality. He shows us how to live in the context of things as they really are.

Biblical writers use language to describe the human condition that is sometimes considered outdated or unfashionable today, but these words and ideas have tremendous value if they accurately describe what is going on inside of us, if they point us to something true about our situation. Let's look at some these ideas and see if they are consistent with our own experience and need.

## The Problem Called "Sin"

What one usually encounters today in a discussion about "sin" is a rather sanitized view of things. Sin is usually jokingly related to whatever is fun, enjoyable, or pleasurable—so that God can be nothing but a kill-joy for condemning it. In religious circles, it is often described as "missing the mark," based on a literal translation of the Greek word. We miss the mark by a little bit, don't quite hit the bull's-eye. It doesn't sound particularly terrible or devastating. But God hates sin for a reason.

Sin is any departure from the life God intends for us. It is a refusal of his call. It is both a cause and an expression of spiritual deadness and blindness. It is plunging past the safe line, over the guardrail God has laid down for us, into great peril physically, emotionally, and spiritually. It is the root cause of all death. And sin lies at the core of the more obvious problems of life, including our fear, loneliness, isolation, guilt, shame, and lack of purpose and meaning.

The prologue of the Bible describes sin's impact. Imagine the unspoiled beauty of the world in which

Adam and Eve lived. We enjoyed unfettered fellowship and intimacy with God. In our wholeness we experienced no shame. "The man and his wife were both naked, and they felt no shame" (Gen. 2:25). Sin shattered all of this. The natural tendency of the sin-damaged soul is to run from God. The first thing Adam and Eve did after sinning was to cover their nakedness and hide from God (Gen. 3:7–8).

We are all runaways. No longer trusting our loving Creator to give us the best possible life, we have each taken things into our own hands. We leave our home in God with a profound sense of personal control, but our rebellion is a one-way path to the pigpen in which the prodigal son in Jesus' parable finds himself. Some of our pigpens are more sophisticated and appear more acceptable than others. But they all infect us with the same deadness of spirit and loss of purpose and meaning.

In Jesus' story, we are told that when the prodigal son "came to his senses" he remembered his father (Luke 15:17). We can live as we want, but we all have those moments of awareness that something is very wrong, that we are lost and have wandered far from home.

Sin leads to worshipping idols of our own making. We are created in such a way that we will worship someone or something. In his commentary on Romans, Paul Achtemeier writes, "The root of our problem is the human propensity to put non-gods in the place of God. Such idolatry clearly means the rejection of the Creator for a deity more pliable to our wishes. Basically, idolatry means *not trusting God to be the kind of God we can live with.*"[2] The tragedy of such idolatry is the exchange of the loving, benevolent lordship of the God who created us for the lordship of something less than God—something that is not only incapable of meeting our needs, but which may ultimately destroy us.

It is not only our communion with God that is destroyed in the fall. We also witness the damaging of the relationship between husband and wife as blame and contention become a part of their experience (Gen. 3:11–13), as well as murder and envy between their children (Gen. 4:1–9). Relationship with self is damaged as Adam and Eve experience guilt and shame for the first time, causing them to cover their nakedness and to hide themselves (Gen. 3:7–8). And their relationship with the created order is disrupted as human disobedience leads to a disharmonious relationship with the land, which now yields weeds and thorns and proves more difficult to work (Gen. 3:17–19 and 4:11–12). Sin has cosmic consequences causing all of creation to long to be "liberated from its bondage to decay" (Rom. 8:21). To put it simply, sin is a force destructive of relationship.

Sin makes life ugly. It destroys relationships and it destroys lives. It is at the root of all that is revolting and disturbing in the world.

There is no kindness in minimizing sin or its effects, because in doing so we fail to warn others of its destructive potential. As Dietrich Bonhoeffer wrote in *Life Together*, "Nothing can be more cruel than the tenderness that consigns another to his sin. Nothing can be more compassionate than the severe rebuke that calls a brother back from the path of sin."[3] O. Hobart Mowrer, writing as a psychologist to psychologists, explains the importance of acknowledging the reality of sin:

> Recovery (constructive change, redemption) is most assuredly attained, not by helping a person reject and rise above his sins, but by helping him *accept them*. This is the paradox which we have not at all understood and which is the very crux of the problem. Just so long as a person lives under the shadow of real, unacknowledged, and unexpiated guilt, he *cannot* (if he has any character at all) "accept himself"; and all *our* efforts to reassure and accept him will avail nothing. He will continue to hate himself and to suffer the inevitable consequences of self-hatred. But the moment he (with or without "assistance") begins to accept his guilt and sinfulness, the possibility of radical reformation opens up; and with this, the individual may legitimately, though not without pain and effort, pass from deep, pervasive self-rejection and self-torture to a new freedom, of self-respect and peace.[4]

# Sin and Death

With sin comes death. We choose independence from God without realizing that the choice is fatal. Like a deep-sea diver disconnecting her oxygen line or a patient in critical condition shutting off his own life support, the biblical picture is one of human delusion about our ability to be self-sustaining. Paul tells us that the natural consequence of our choice to separate ourselves from God's life-giving authority is our own physical and spiritual death (Rom. 6:23).

And with death comes a sense of fear and dread. Death is what William James has called "the worm at the core" of our best efforts at happiness. "We need a life not correlated with death," James wrote, "a health not liable to illness, a kind of good that will not perish, a good in fact that flies beyond the Goods of nature."[5] Ernest Becker's *The Denial of Death* provides a penetrating look at our innate terror of death and our incessant efforts to escape the burden of this fear. Death represents loss, forfeiture, a realization of our limits. It symbolizes the inadmissible reality of our lack of control over so much of life. "The idea of death, the fear of it, haunts the human animal like nothing else; it is a mainspring of human activity—activity designed largely to avoid the fatality of death, to overcome it by denying in some way that it is the final destiny for man."[6]

The Nobel Prize winner George Wald at age 69 wrote, "I have never seen a person die. I have never even been in the same house while a person died. How about birth? An obstetrician invited me to see my first birth only last year. Just think, these are the greatest events of life and they have been taken out of our experience. We somehow hope to live full emotional lives when we have carefully expunged the sources of the deepest human emotions."[7] We are not equipped to face the question of our own death, so generally we do not.

When I was younger I thought for some time that I had worked through my fear of death. During college

I took a job as an orderly in a hospital. Part of my work involved moving the bodies of those who had died in the emergency room to the morgue. I remember a pleasant woman in her fifties, with short blonde hair, coming into the ER describing the chest pain that had started during dinner. She was energetic and full of life. Three hours later she was dead. Actually experiencing death, seeing the lifelessness of those who had been so animated hours earlier, invoked in me a forceful sense of my own longing to live and a corresponding dread of death. I was forced to face my feelings about my own mortality. The fear of death is not an invention of modern philosophy. It is a core human reality:

> But we do see Jesus, who was made lower than the angels for a little while, now crowned with glory and honor because he suffered death, so that by the grace of God he might taste death for everyone.... Since the children have flesh and blood, he too shared in their humanity so that by his death he might break the power of him who holds the power of death—that is, the devil—and free those who all their lives were held in slavery by their fear of death. (Heb. 2:9, 14–15)

# An Ongoing Battle

There is something else about the human condition we need to understand if we are to make sense of the story in which we live. Our souls have an enemy. We live our lives in the context of an all-out battle. Jesus began his ministry by doing combat with the enemy (Luke 4:1–2). Satan was likewise involved in the events leading to the crucifixion (Luke 22:3). He wanted Jesus dead. Paul indicated that it was stupidity on the part of the forces of evil to assume this strategy. By inviting Jesus into the realm of death they orchestrated their own demise (1 Cor. 2:8). Jesus saw his death as part of a spiritual battle and essential to victory (John 12:31–32). He descended to hell, into the kingdom of death, the core of Satan's power, dealing a crushing and definitive blow to the enemy. Not only did he walk out victorious, in his kindness he now invites all of us to participate in his victory by walking out of the jaws of death with him (1 Peter 3:18–22; Eph. 4:9–10). Jesus is currently working to bring to completion the ramifications of the lethal blow he dealt the enemy through his death and resurrection (1 Cor. 15:24–26). He invites us to participate in the victory, pushing out the borders of the kingdom through faith, proclamation of the good news, and prayer (Eph. 6:11–12).

This is the story the Bible was written to tell. And we cannot understand the nature of our lives without understanding the nature of the conflict in which we find ourselves.

## God's Response to Our Need

Recently, through a miraculous set of circumstances our family was blessed with a new son. We had been considering adopting, but only five days before the birth of our son we were contacted by a friend who is an adoption attorney about a baby who was about to be born and needed a home. We decided in minutes that we would be his family. The bonding that usually unfolds over nine months occurred in our hearts so quickly. I did not know what to expect, but before we ever saw him we loved him deeply. I was stunned by what was happening in my own heart. As we awaited his delivery at the hospital, we experienced anxiety, joy, and the same vast array of emotions we felt while awaiting the birth of our biological children. From the moment of his birth, when we first laid eyes on him, we fell head over heels in love with him. Our other children embraced him immediately. Aaron brought out the best in them because they loved him. We were all amazed at how a helpless, speechless infant could channel so many tons of love and joy into our lives. I quickly formed the kinds of dreams born of love, envisioning a future shaped by grace and an environment of love.

After thirty-three days the birth mother decided that she would attempt to raise him and we were required to let him go.

The pain and grief have been tremendous. Nobody could have prepared me for how painful this loss would be. Our hearts are still raw. Sometimes at night I am awakened by the silence, remembering and longing to hear his little noises. In our loss we constantly think of Aaron with great longing. We think of what might have been. We think of the experiences of his development we are missing. We remember the feeling of holding him and kissing him. We are slowly moving forward, but we will always love him, always miss him, always pray.

I share this part of our lives because for me it provides a glimpse into God's heart. To an infinitely greater degree than I long for a relationship with Aaron, God desires a relationship with every one of us. Peter said that God longs for "everyone to come to repentance" (2 Peter 3:9). Taken seriously, Jesus' parables of the lost sheep, the lost coin, and the lost son recorded in Luke 15 reveal that God is grieved by our running from him and longs for renewed relationship. God pursues us with passion and rejoices with all of heaven when any of us returns home. Jesus said to a sincere seeker named Nicodemus, "For God so loved the world that he gave his one and only Son, that whoever believes in him shall not perish but have eternal life" (John 3:16).

We lost something at Eden when relationship with God was broken. To face ourselves honestly, we must come to recognize that the problem with the world is not something out there—not some ideology, political movement, or impersonal force—but something within us. I have had to come to terms with the fact that *I* am the problem. The brokenness and pain in the world are there precisely because of the brokenness within every human heart—including my own. The duplicity within my heart is a reflection of all that is wrong with the world. But this did not stop God from loving us.

Despite this deep love, however, God had a problem. He could not simply overlook sin. There was a terrific price that had to be paid to secure an answer to our dilemma. He could not solve the problem with a message or a set of instructions alone. A mere emissary would not do. One of the things that sets Christianity apart from other religions is God's initiative. Other religions may describe a path for us to follow that is supposed to enable us to connect with God or the eternal dimension of reality. The Christian message is that God himself comes seeking us in the person of Jesus Christ. Through his life, ministry, sin-bearing death, and resurrection, Jesus has done all that is necessary to restore us to our relationship with God.

Only Jesus can see us safely home. Only he can return us to the arms of our Father where we will find the answers to the deepest needs and longings of our hearts. If we will come to him trusting and believing, he can give us life that is really life. The life that he promises, eternal life, is not a future acquisition that awaits us some day—it begins today. It is eternal life because it has no end. The Bible not only describes our unending life with God, but it teaches us how to live here and now, today. Jesus said, "I have come that they may have life, and have it to the full" (John 10:10).

The choice to follow Jesus is the most essential step on the path of learning to fully and freely love as God intended.

# –Making Love Real–

Our focus has been on fully and accurately understanding our real condition and the magnitude of our problem—what the Bible describes as sin, separation from God, and spiritual death. Spend some time today thinking about what Jesus has done for you, how he answers your deepest needs.

The prophet Isaiah wrote about Jesus that "he took up our pain and bore our suffering.... and by his wounds we are healed" (Isa. 53:4–5). Focus on the places of greatest pain and brokenness in your life. Invite Jesus into those places and welcome his healing. In recognizing our problem, it is helpful to recognize that there is also hope. If you have never made the decision to follow Jesus, call out to him right now. Tell him about your need. Welcome his forgiveness and grace. Paul wrote, "As Scripture says, 'Anyone who believes in him will never be put to shame.' ... For, 'Everyone who calls on the name of the Lord will be saved'" (Rom. 10:11, 13).

# 3

# The Crucial Connection: Dependence

❧

I was carrying our newborn son, Jonathan, down lacquered wood stairs in stocking feet when all of a sudden my feet shot out from under me. With no time to plan my fall, all I could think about was the safety of the baby. This mission was accomplished with an awkward and inglorious crash landing on my backside. I was paralyzed briefly with excruciating pain. Feelings of unmitigated helplessness filled the moment. The baby was still asleep on my chest. Carole rushed to the sound of the crash calling out, "Is the baby okay?" She took the baby with a curious look emanating the unspoken question, "What in the world were you doing?" I was content to be alone in my pain as I decided how long I should lie there before attempting to get up. The church staff was on the way over for breakfast. When the doorbell finally rang, I got up and hobbled to the door, never saying a word about my recent adventure. The only sympathy I would receive was from my doctor, who later agreed they were some of the most impressive bruises he had seen.

I never enjoy feeling helpless. I'll let other people help me as long as I don't feel completely helpless. The moment I feel truly helpless I reflexively want to establish my independence again. When my pride is challenged I have a hard time accepting help.

I have also noticed that the more helpless I feel, the more simple my prayers become. Sometimes when I feel most helpless I can hardly get beyond the words, "Help, Lord." O. Hallesby explains in his book *Prayer* that "prayer is something deeper than words. It is present in the soul before it has been formulated in words. And it abides in the soul after the last words of prayer have passed over our lips." Paul described this phenomenon by saying, "We do not know what we ought to pray for, but the Spirit himself intercedes for us through wordless groans" (Rom. 8:26). Hallesby writes that the most essential element in a vital life of prayer is *a sense of helplessness*. "Your helplessness is your best prayer. It calls from your heart to the heart of God with greater effect than all your uttered pleas. He hears it from the moment you are seized with helplessness, and he becomes actively engaged at once in hearing and answering the prayer of your helplessness."[1]

Helplessness may not seem like a positive virtue in this world. If atheistic evolution accurately describes the world, we are thrown into an endless battle of competition and comparison where dependence can only be construed as weakness. But if Jesus is right and the physical universe is the possession of our trustworthy Father, then dependence is not only a virtue but essential to life in the kingdom of God. It's no wonder then that, in the final moments of his life, Jesus invited his disciples to a life of utter and absolute dependence on him.

## Dependence Is a Matter of Life and Death

Jesus' words and actions on the evening before his death provide us with essential insight regarding what it means to follow him. If the whole of our spiritual life grows out of our connection with Jesus and dependence on him, then learning to "abide" in him is essential to being filled and possessed by love.

Jesus said, "Remain in me, as I also remain in you. No branch can bear fruit by itself; it must remain in the vine.... If you do not remain in me, you are like a branch that is thrown away and withers" (John 15:4, 6). God is the creator and the source of all life. To be connected to God is to have life, and to be separated from God is to have no life.

The illusion of autonomy is at the core of our problem. Yet this sense of autonomy is part of my everyday life. I move through the day rarely aware of my dependence, actually believing that I am moving, breathing, living, acting on my own. Beginning in the garden, the human race chose independence from God without recognizing that the choice was fatal. The same sin continues today. We are absolutely dependent on God; and most of the time, we don't see it at all.

Creation has patterns of dependence woven into its very fabric. A massive California redwood is no less dependent on the soil in which it is rooted than the delicate poppy. All living things have a minimal environment essential to life. Yet as humans we strive for independence without realizing that we, too, have a minimal environment essential to life. For us that environment includes relationship with God.

While I was giving blood at a Red Cross blood bank, a nurse drawing blood from another patient said to the nurse taking care of me, "Take two units from that guy, he can spare it." I am six feet six inches, and she apparently thought I carried a backup unit or two. My nurse was the better physiologist. She said, "Actually he needs more blood to keep his motor running." It doesn't really matter our size and strength. We are all dependent, and we remain dependent on the God.

## Dependence Is Essential to Fruitfulness

A second great theme reflected in Jesus' words was that *apart from God there is no fruitfulness*. Jesus said, "Remain in me, as I also remain in you. No branch can bear fruit by itself; it must remain in the vine. Neither can you bear fruit unless you remain in me. I am the vine; you are the branches. If you remain in me and I in you, you will bear much fruit; apart from me you can do nothing" (John 15:4–5). Our tendency is to think of fruitfulness as a matter of hard work, giftedness, and capability. But Jesus made it clear that fruitfulness is a by-product of an intimate relationship with him.

The job of the branch is to remain attached to the vine. That's it. We don't work, strain, produce, or struggle. It is our part simply to remain connected, to abide in Christ. It is only as we remain attached to Jesus that fruitfulness is possible.

Early in his ministry Hudson Taylor, the pioneering missionary to the interior of China (and one of my heroes since childhood), struggled with a constant sense of frustration over his lack of spiritual growth and development. At age thirty-seven he explained his longing for change in a letter to his mother:

> My own position becomes continually more and more responsible, and my need greater of special grace to fill it; but I have continually to mourn that I follow at such a distance and learn so slowly to imitate my precious Master. I cannot tell you how I am buffeted sometimes by temptation. I never knew how bad a heart I had.... Often I am tempted to think that one so full of sin cannot be a child of God at all.[2]

My heart tracks with Taylor's word for word—I'm slow to learn, I'm easily tempted, I'm following Jesus at a distance.

During this period of discouragement Taylor received a letter from another missionary, John McCarthy, who had heard about Taylor's struggle. McCarthy describes a recent breakthrough in his life:

> Abiding, not striving nor struggling; looking off unto Him; trusting Him for present power; trusting Him to subdue all inward corruption; resting in the love of an almighty Savior, in the conscious joy of a complete salvation, a salvation "from all sin" (this is His Word); willing that His will should truly be supreme—this is not new, and yet 'tis new to me. I feel as though the first dawning of a glorious day had risen upon me. I hail it with trembling, yet with trust. I seem to have got to the edge only, but of a sea which is boundless; to have sipped only, but of that which fully satisfies. Christ literally all seems to me now the power, the only power for service; the only ground for unchanging joy. May He lead us into the realization of His unfathomable fullness.[3]

The letter changed Taylor's life forever. From that point on, the great theme of Taylor's spiritual journey was abiding in Christ. Writing to his sister in England, Taylor reflected on his experience:

> As I thought of the vine and the branches, what light the blessed Spirit poured direct into my soul! How great seemed my mistake in having wished to get the sap, the fullness out of Him. I saw not only that Jesus would never leave me, but that I was a member of His body, of His flesh and His bones. The vine is not the root merely, but all—root, stem, branches, twigs, leaves, flowers, fruit: And Jesus is not only that: He is soil and sunshine, air and showers, and ten thousand times more than we have ever dreamed, wished for, or needed....

> I am no better than before (may I not say, in a sense, I
> do not wish to be, nor am I striving to be) but I am dead
> and buried with Christ—aye, and risen too and ascended;
> and now Christ lives in me.[4]

In the physical realm our development follows a predictable path. We are infants carried in our parents' arms, we learn to crawl, then walk, then run, and if we are clever we may even find a way to fly. Yet Isaiah describes our spiritual development quite differently: "But those who hope in the LORD will renew their strength. They will soar on wings like eagles; they will run and not grow weary, they will walk and not be faint" (Isa. 40:31). Our spiritual development follows a direction opposite to our physical development. We fly at first, set off on our way by tastes of God's love which seem overwhelming to us. Soon we settle to the ground and run with great zeal. Then we learn to walk, sometimes too fast getting ahead, sometimes too slow falling behind. With time we learn the Master's pace and we walk side by side with him, learning from him. In the difficult times he carries us and when we are old and mature we are cradled in his arms as if an infant, wanting only to see his face and nothing else.

This is the posture of the mature and fruitful, the posture of dependence. In the language of psychology we tend to think of maturity as moving toward independence, but in the spiritual realm the opposite is true. Maturity involves dependence—absolute dependence on God and healthy interdependence in relationships with people.

# Dependence on God Is Foundational to Character

A third aspect of our dependence on God taken up in Christ's analogy of the vine and branches is the idea that *apart from God there is no virtue*. "If you remain in me and my words remain in you, ask whatever you wish, and it will be done for you. This is to my Father's glory, that you bear much fruit, showing yourselves to be my disciples" (John 15:7–8). The result of abiding in Christ, of walking closely with him and doing the things that he says, is a changed character. We will think differently, live differently, even pray differently and with greater authority. We will experience his love, joy, and constant friendship (see John 15:9–15).

It's possible to follow Jesus for ten, twenty, thirty years and begin to feel a sense of confidence about our own ability to walk independently, in our own strength. We face some previously defeated problem or temptation and we say to ourselves, "I can handle this situation. I've done it a hundred times before." Jesus is saying something very different. It doesn't matter if we've followed him for thirty or forty years. We're as dependent upon the grace of God today for the way we live as we were the moment we first trusted him.

As a leader I fear my abilities at least as much as I fear my areas of weakness. If I recognize a weakness it can be a place where God's strength reveals itself. If I depend upon my strengths rather than on Jesus my weaknesses will begin to do their damage to me and the people around me. I must depend on him, not myself.

I have heard it said that Christianity is nothing but a crutch for the weak. My objection to that metaphor is that it's not strong enough! Christianity is more than simply a crutch. It's a lifeline to the drowning, it's oxygen to the suffocating, it's life support to the dying, it's hope for the hopeless, it's salvation for the broken and lost. When the illusion of self-sufficiency blinds us, God gets pushed to the periphery. But when our eyes are opened once again to our state of helplessness, we find our way back to depending on God—which is the very life he always intended for us.

The typical Christian life can feel like walking a tightrope. We try to get from point A to point B by constructing a narrow rope of our own making—a rope woven out of our education, accomplishments, finances, family, relationships, and whatever else we consider to be an expression of our own strength. But inevitably something happens—an unexpected illness, a family tragedy, a problem in a relationship that falls apart. All of a sudden that rope snaps, and we are falling through the air. That's where God comes in. He's the safety net. He catches us; he keeps us from falling to the ground. We rely on him for a while, until we get back on our feet; and then we start weaving our tightrope all over again.

But that's not a biblical picture of the Christian life. In reality, God is the tightrope and the net and the whole structure and the only way to get from point A to point B.

# An Invitation to Friendship

Helen Keller wrote of her teacher and lifelong friend, Anne Sullivan, after her death:

> My teacher is so near to me that I scarcely think of myself apart from her. How much of my delight in all beautiful things is innate, and how much is due to her influence, I can never tell. I feel that her being is inseparable from my own, and that the footsteps of my life are in hers. All the best of me belongs to her—there is not a talent, or an inspiration or a joy in me that has not been awakened by her loving touch.[5]

Jesus invites us to such a relationship. "As the Father has loved me, so have I loved you. Now remain in my love" (John 15:9). Only in a relationship of dependence on Jesus—a life inseparable from his, our footsteps in his, when all that is best about us is him, where our hearts are awakened by his touch—will we learn to love.

Jesus invites us to "remain in his love." He is asking us to sink our roots deep down into the things of God, and to give God a chance to help us grow. Emotional and spiritual health requires dependence on him. We cannot be filled with his life and his love without absolute dependence on him.

When our children were small I would take them by the hand and we would run side by side. I held their hands firmly. Before long we would come to a point, because of our relative masses, where their feet would barely touch the ground. They would sail along, feet touching lightly every fifth or sixth step, squealing with delight. Carole never liked it when I did this. She wanted to know what was going to happen if I lost hold of their hands. Psalm 37:24 tells us that when those who live in friendship with God fall, they will not fall on their faces, because God is the one who holds them by the hand. He is able to take care of you. He is up to the challenge.

One of the great privileges of practicing family medicine is the experience of delivering babies. Part of the delivery is in simplest terms "the catch." On a birthing table there is a sheer drop from the edge of the table to the floor below. I have been told that in some medical schools a story is told of a student who dropped a baby. I suspect that such stories may be legends kept alive to inspire fear about the importance of catching the baby. During the first few deliveries of a new intern the supervising resident or attending makes it clear that you have to get hold of that baby.

When I'm delivering a baby and the head begins to crown, the rest of the world fades away into oblivion and things seem to go into slow motion. At the moment of birth every ounce of my focus and attention is given to the safe arrival of the baby. The entire universe is right there at the edge of the table—that little baby, a new life entering the world. It is always an experience of profound emotion and joy. That precious life has my undivided attention.

God is like that in his relationship with us. At

every moment of our lives we have his undivided attention. He doesn't miss a thing. Jesus said, "Are not two sparrows sold for a penny? Yet not one of them will fall to the ground outside your Father's care. And even the very hairs of your head are all numbered. So don't be afraid" (Matt. 10:29–31). He is up to the job of our trust. He's here for us right now. We can depend on him.

## –Making Love Real–

Write out a list of the three or four struggles that weigh on you the most—the things that occupy your mind when you are quiet and still. Actively give these things to God. Ask for him to take control. Be honest with him about your inability to fix everything. Consciously choose to depend on him.

This will require you to trust and to take a risk. When you feel like taking back control from God, remember: Exercising trust and learning dependence on Christ are essential to growing your capacity for love.

# 4

# Keeping First Things First: Longing

＊＊＊

As a medical resident, rare, brief periods of sleep at night in the hospital were often punctuated by an overhead page calling a "code blue," summoning us to the room of a patient in cardiac or respiratory arrest. A team of a dozen highly trained individuals interacted in an orchestrated effort to save the life of a patient. My job was usually to insert a flexible plastic tube down the trachea between the vocal cords to provide a protected airway, and to "call the code," giving orders coordinating the efforts of the team.

In a medical emergency like that, the most basic things are the most important. All physicians and emergency personnel are taught to remember the basics, literally called the ABCs—A. Airway, B. Breathing,

C. Circulation—things crucial to life that must be instinctively remembered in any endeavor to sustain life.

Breathing is so basic to life that we literally cannot help but breathe. We breathe when we are asleep. We can hold our breath to a point, but we will either become so overwhelmed by our hunger for oxygen that we start to breathe or we will pass out and, once unconscious, reflexively begin to breathe. Only a severe metabolic derangement or the alteration or suppression of our central nervous system can stop our drive to breathe.

Spiritually, we are wired in such a way that the natural, deepest longing of the human spirit is a longing and a hunger for God. God is to the human spirit what oxygen is to the body. Our spirits long to be filled with God just as our bodies long to fill our lungs with air. The often-quoted Westminster Shorter Catechism expresses the ultimate goal of this desire: "Man's chief end is to glorify God and enjoy Him forever." C. S. Lewis wrote, "A car is made to run on gasoline, and it would not run properly on anything else. Now God designed the human machine to run on himself. He himself is the fuel our spirits were designed to burn, or the food our spirits were designed to feed on. There is no other."[1]

# The Importance of Our Hunger for God

Jesus, resting at Jacob's well, initiated a conversation with a Samaritan woman who came to draw water

(John 4:1–42). She came at noon while the sun was high and hot to avoid contact with her neighbors. She was a woman with a reputation. She had felt the sting of derisive stares and heard the muttering of neighbors talking behind her back. She had carefully isolated herself within the community.

Jesus understood the situation. Couched in a metaphor he held out the cup of grace. While asking for a drink of water, Jesus said to her, "If you knew the gift of God and who it is that asks you for a drink, you would have asked him and he would have given you *living water*" (John 4:10). By referring to living water Jesus is talking about the spiritual ABCs, the things that touch us at our core and have the capacity to meet our deepest needs. "Everyone who drinks this water will be thirsty again, but those who drink *the water I give* them will never thirst. Indeed, *the water I give them will become in them a spring of water welling up to eternal life*" (John 4:13–14).

The most basic of our spiritual faculties is hunger and thirst, reflected in our physical hunger for food and our thirst for water. We are spiritual beings created by God, in the image of God, for relationship with God. The ability to tap into our innate spiritual appetite and to recognize its importance is crucial to our spiritual well-being. So Jesus addressed this woman at the level of her spiritual hunger.

Like the woman at the well, we are each created with great desire and longing. Desire drives us, animates us, and shapes the direction of our lives. It is

God who gives us our desires as well as fulfills them. David wrote, "You open your hand and satisfy the desires of every living thing" (Ps. 145:16; see v. 19 also). To repress our longings or to minimize desire is not the same as experiencing fulfillment. In fact it seems to me that God draws us to himself by means of our deepest desires.

Throughout creation, God has purposefully designed objects that both satisfy and delight. Think about an orange. Why does it exist at all? Superfluous to the operation of the universe, yet so wholly appealing to human senses. God designed the orange for his own delight, but also for ours. The skin with its multiple shades of orange, brilliance, and sheen; as the skin is broken, microvesicles explode giving way to a fine mist, cool, fragrant, and refreshing; the fleshy fruit filled with juice both sweet and tart, appealing to the taste buds. The entire process of eating an orange is satisfying, nourishing, and refreshing. Creation could be monochromatic and all foods taste the same. But it's not. God not only finds delight in his creation, he delights in giving us delight.

In the context of this God-bathed and delight-filled world Jesus instructs us: "Ask and it will be given to you; seek and you will find; knock and the door will be opened to you" (Matt. 7:7). In Christianity the goal is not the repression of desire as in some religions or "desirelessness" as in Buddhism, but the pursuit of our desires in the direction set for them by God.

# What Happened to Our Appetite?

A severe alteration or dysfunction of our central nervous system can cause us to lose our urge to breathe. The same kind of thing can happen to us spiritually. We can lose our hunger for God. The Samaritan woman had an appetite dysfunction. Jesus sought to expose her need in order to facilitate healing and restoration. Jesus asked her to go and get her husband. She replied that she had no husband. Jesus pushed forward assertively. "You are right when you say you have no husband. The fact is, you have had five husbands, and the man you now have is not your husband. What you have just said is quite true" (John 4:17–18). For two people who met only minutes earlier they quickly got down to the nitty-gritty. Jesus sensed the urgency of her situation and stuck to the ABCs. Jesus recognized when he met this woman that something was broken inside of her—the same way he recognizes the brokenness inside each of us. There was a hunger in her not satisfied by anything she had tried. The life she had chosen wasn't working.

Many yearnings of the human soul are ultimately spiritual. When answers to our spiritual longings are not found in the course of our day-to-day lives we find ourselves seeking answers in all the wrong places. M. Scott Peck writes that those lost in compulsive, driven pursuit of sex are in fact looking for spirituality. Malcolm Muggeridge describes sex as the mysticism of the materialist. There is a relationship between this woman's longing for a relationship with a man and her hunger for God. Thus, Jesus offered the woman at the well the opportunity to have her deep longing filled up by tasting of the spiritual water only he could give. He alone can permanently and completely take away our sense of emptiness.

What happens to our hunger for God? How does our hunger for the most essential things get diverted? How do we come to a place where we confuse our spiritual longings with other appetites?

## The Cause of the Dysfunction and Confusion

Just as there is an outer world that begins at the eye and proceeds seemingly infinitely outward, so there is an inner world that begins at the eye and proceeds inwardly into a vast, tumultuous, almost endless, and complex realm. This inner world determines a lot about who we really are. Jesus said it is the things that come from within, out of our hearts, that have the power to destroy us (Mark 7:14–23) and that the best indicator of spiritual health and the real condition of our hearts is our devotion to loving God and people (Matt. 22:36–40). The matters of our inner world are the things that concerned Jesus most.

Paul taught that the disruption of our inner world begins with sin—that is, our rejection of God—a choice that leads to the corruption of our minds and hearts (Rom. 1:21). Displacing God from our hearts as the source of satisfaction for our deepest hunger and as the primary recipient of our devoted love leads to dysfunction in all of our appetites and desires—producing a variety of problems in all of our relationships (Rom. 1:24–31).

Paul also pointed out that we have a hard time facing our real condition and typically react with "stubbornness" and an "unrepentant heart" (Rom. 2:5). Our denial takes many forms. The chaos of our inner life can be repressed by the sedating, numbing effects of all sorts of addictive attachments—food, alcohol, entertainment, television, materialism, accomplishment, busyness, drugs, and the misuse of our sexuality, to name a few. Since these things cannot satisfy our souls as God does, they tend to be abused rather than enjoyed. They often become the focal point of an escalating cycle of dependence that eventually consumes us. John Piper writes, "The greatest enemy of hunger for God is not poison but apple pie. It is not the banquet of the wicked that dulls our appetite for heaven, but endless nibbling at the table of the world. It is not the X-rated video, but the primetime dribble of triviality we drink in every night."[2]

I have found that if I keep busy enough I can avoid thinking about some of the unpleasantness lurking beneath the surface. But the problems within bubble up and bleed through into my speech and actions and eventually affect my life at every level.

If we remove the sedating effects of our self-absorption and self-indulgence through stillness, quiet, prayer, fasting, and other spiritual disciplines, we will experience the symptoms of our appetite dysfunction more fully. Frustration, impulsivity, worry, anxiety, fear, and most certainly anger will all rise to the surface, revealing the true condition our heart had been in all along. Such insight into your inner self can certainly be shocking. But it is only when we strip away the props and defenses long enough to face the darkness within that the possibility of new life can emerge.

If we courageously and honestly face the problems within and let God prove his love for us even where our hearts are messiest, then his healing and transformation will come. We will discover that buried beneath the pile of our sin, addictions, and self-absorption lies our true hunger—our hunger for God. When that appetite is restored and fulfilled by God himself, a renewed passion and capacity for loving God and other people comes alive in our hearts.

## Putting First Things First

Cultivating a hunger and longing for God is essential to the growth of love. We function as God intends us to when we allow God to fill the void within and learn to love him passionately. When we love God above all else, our capacity for love grows in all of our relationships. C. S. Lewis said at the end of a letter to a friend, "When I have learnt to love God better than my earthly dearest, I shall love my earthly dearest better than I do now. In so far as I learn to love my earthly dearest at the expense of God and *instead* of God, I shall be moving towards the state in which I shall not love my earthly dearest at all. When first things are put first, second things are not suppressed but increased."[3]

Throughout the Gospels, what Jesus tried to teach us about life in his kingdom is that for *everything* we have only *God*. During his temptation, Jesus told Satan that there was more to this life than just meeting his own temporal needs. And to the woman at the well he said that no matter how much she drank she would always thirst again—until she drank of the water that is God.

Later, when the disciples returned from town with food in hand, they encouraged Jesus to eat something. But he said, "I have food to eat that you know nothing about.... My food ... is to do the will of him who sent me and to finish his work" (John 4:32, 34). True satisfaction in life comes from staying connected to God, feasting on his presence, and following his lead from moment to moment. We were created to live on bread the world knows nothing of.

The world is starved for compassion—for true, unselfish, lasting, growing love. Such love begins by cultivating a deeper relationship with God—one in which our souls are satisfied by him alone. Only then can his endless love be poured through our lives into a famished world. When our hearts and minds are filled with the kindness, goodness, and beauty of God, the natural inclination of our hearts—that is, our *hunger* and our *food*—will be to do the will of him who created us and sends us as his emissaries into the world.

# —Making Love Real—

Every day we face a drone of noise and a barrage of images and ideas from a busy world clamoring for our attention. Part of placing our focus on Jesus involves resisting the pressures by which the world tries to squeeze us into its mold (see Rom. 12:1–2 PH). When are you quiet and still enough to notice what is going on in your heart? When do you consciously give God time to speak?

Plan a half-day retreat sometime in the next two to three weeks. Get alone with God and be quiet. Bring a Bible and a journal. Read God's Word and let him speak to your heart. Be open about what is going on inside. Be honest with him about your struggles and your desires. Open the whole of your life to him in prayer. Listen. And follow.

# 5

# Recognizing Love's Source: Openness

Y ou were made for love. This truth reveals itself in human nature in a number of ways. We are all created with a need to be loved. Being loved is essential to our health, well-being, and development. We function best when we know we are loved. And we are created with a tremendous capacity for loving others.

But what exactly is love? Where does love come from? How do we give and receive it? The first few chapters of this book have addressed some foundational ideas necessary to a thoughtful answer to these questions— grasping the true source of our value and significance, an accurate assessment of our condition and need, understanding the nature and extent of our dependence on God, and the revitalization of our spiritual hunger.

First Corinthians 13, often referred to as "the Love Chapter," offers a concise, practical, hands-on, working definition of love. Though lofty and idealistic in its listing of simple absolutes, it leaves no question in our minds as to what love looks like when we find it. The other love chapter in the New Testament is 1 John 4, a theological treatise on love that directly addresses the question of love's origin.

## Where Does Love Come From?

"Love comes from God" (1 John 4:7). The idea that all love originates with God is simple enough—all things originate with God—but the implications of this fact are not so easy to grasp. It is easier to conceive of some emotional reservoir or mechanism inside each of us that produces love, functioning better at certain times than others. But that is never the argument of Scripture. John lays out the biblical case in seven simple ideas, answering the question of love's source.

*God is love.* Twice in this chapter, John uses the phrase, "God is love" (1 John 4:8, 16). For God, love isn't just something that he does; it's an aspect of who he is. There are only a few ontological statements—expressions of what God is in his essence—in the New Testament. In John 4 Jesus says, "God is spirit"; in 1 John 1, "God is light"; and in 1 John 4, "God is love." As Otto Weber writes, "God is in his essence, his reality, holy, free sovereign love. In its shortest form, this is the Christian concept of God."[1]

An erroneous idea I hear repeated periodically suggests that God created us because he was lonely. He was out there by himself and he needed someone to talk with, someone with whom he could have a relationship. Nothing could be further from truth about God's character. God did not need to create us. God in and of himself is the most joyful and fulfilled being in the universe. There is no need in God. In *The Four Loves*, C. S. Lewis wrote, "In God there is no hunger that needs to be filled, only plenteousness that desires to give." It is his nature to give of himself. He gave life to us, even though he knew the terrific cost he must pay to redeem us. As Lewis pointed out, "God, who needs nothing, loves into existence wholly superfluous creatures in order that he may love and perfect them."[2]

*"Love comes from God."* All of the love you have to give away, you received ultimately from God. All love comes from God (1 John 4:7).

Our capacity for love is a "common grace." By that I mean that not only followers of Jesus are able to love. People without a relationship with God may also demonstrate a tremendous capacity for loving others. Jesus said that God allows the rain to fall on the just and the unjust (Matt. 5:45). In the same way John says that our capacity for love is something that was given to us as a gift from God. What the New Testament does argue is that followers of Jesus ought to be the most loving people, demonstrating a growing and ever-deepening capacity for love as they experience the love of God and are connected with the life of God. In fact, even our love for God comes from God himself.

*Love is practical.* "This is how God showed his love among us: He sent his one and only Son into the world that we might live through him" (1 John 4:9). God took the biggest problem we ever had—the problem of sin and separation from him and our resulting spiritual death—and he found an answer. In his holiness he might have given up on us; in his righteousness he might have snuffed us out; but in his love God redeemed us, without forsaking what was necessary to maintain his holiness and righteousness. God himself paid the terrible price for human sin. He became our servant. Jesus said, "For even the Son of Man did not come to be served, but to serve, and to give his life as a ransom for many" (Mark 10:45).

*God's love is the model of all loves.* Love is not some arbitrary quality that we get to define however we wish. Rather, God's love is the model by which we understand what love is. "This is love: not that we loved God, but that he loved us and sent his Son as an atoning sacrifice for our sins" (1 John 4:10). That's the picture of love. That's what love is all about. God shows us through his own actions what love looks like. Apart from the cross we might never have known what real love looks like.

*God's love is always "prior" to our own.* God does

more than offer a model. In his great humility and gentleness he serves us before he asks us to serve. "Dear friends, since God so loved us, we also ought to love one another" (1 John 4:11). Earlier he wrote, "This is how we know what love is: Jesus Christ laid down his life for us. And we ought to lay down our lives for one another" (1 John 3:16). Why should we live sacrificial lives? Because Jesus Christ laid down his life for us. Why are we to love? Because God loved us. Paul says that we are to forgive one another. Why? Because God in Christ has forgiven us (Eph. 4:32). Why should you be generous in response to the needs of others? Because God has been generous to you (2 Cor. 8:9). Why should you live with humility? God in Christ has already shown himself to be the most humble being in the universe (Phil. 2:6–7).

Because he's Lord, because he's in charge, we might assume God could ask us to do whatever he wants, whether he's done it or not. His humility is demonstrated in his service to us. God never ever asks us to do anything for others that he has not already done for us himself. He asks for our whole heart, and he withholds nothing of himself from us (Rom. 8:32). This is the "priorness" of God's love.

*God's love is transformational.* John describes the impact of being loved by God. "If anyone acknowledges that Jesus is the Son of God, God lives in them and they in God. And so we know and rely on the love God has for us. God is love. Whoever lives in love lives in God, and God in them. This is how love is made complete among us so that we will have confidence on the day of judgment: In this world we are like Jesus. There is no fear in love. But perfect love drives out fear, because fear has to do with punishment. The one who fears is not made perfect in love" (1 John 4:15–18).

There's a logical flow to these verses. It's important to see the development as John described the process of transformation. First of all, we experience God's love for us by entering into a relationship with Jesus Christ by faith. Second, as we find that he is faithful to us and committed to our well-being, we come to "know and rely on the love God has for us." Then as we learn to depend on God's love, "love is made complete among us." This ripened work of his love being made complete leads to "confidence" in our relationship with God and the end of fear. Even when we stand before God in judgment we can be confident. Others may fear, but our hearts will be glad to be with God. As a result, we are becoming more and more like Jesus here and now, "in this world," as we experience the Father's love. We have a growing capacity for love as Jesus' love is being poured out through our lives on a regular basis.

John also described the possible failure of the process. "The one who fears is not made perfect in love" (1 John 4:18). If we are living in fear, it is not a failure of his love for us but an indication of our need to allow his love to permeate our lives. Fear is a manifestation of the places in our lives where we do not feel loved and cared for. Experiencing the full extent of God's love for us brings an end to any fear. His love creates an unshakable environment of trust.

Being loved like that is a transforming experience. The love of God, fully experienced and expressed in our hearts, causes us to become like Jesus at the core of our being.

*We must receive love from beyond ourselves.* John concluded the final paragraph of his treatise with this crucial insight into our capacity for love. "We love because he first loved us" (1 John 4:19). If we are to truly love as God intended we must first receive love from beyond ourselves.

In seeking to love it is not uncommon to skip this step. We start with the command to love. We tell people to love each other. But instructing people to love each other without telling them how much they are loved is like telling people to prepare a meal without groceries. Until we are loved we are like pens without ink, cars without gas, or someone writing checks without making a deposit first. By ourselves we just can't do it. We cannot give what we do not have. If we are to love, we must receive love from beyond ourselves.

When our love does not flow from the well of love God has given, it will be obvious in our relationships. Our ability to be kind, generous, or otherwise loving to others will be lacking. In the end, the way we treat people reflects the condition of our heart in our relationship with God. Human relationships are a mirror in which we view our interior world. Ultimately, *our capacity for love is a reflection of our openness to the love of God.*

# Embracing God's Love

The Bible attributes our newfound confidence in our relationship with God to the work of the Holy Spirit. "We know that we live in him and he in us: He has given us of his Spirit" (1 John 4:13). Paul wrote, "And hope does not put us to shame." Why? "Because God's love has been poured out into our hearts through the Holy Spirit, who has been given to us" (Rom. 5:5). The Holy Spirit is the personal mediator of God's love to human hearts. Abiding in the Holy Spirit and keeping in step with the Spirit are expressions of our dependence on God. As we are filled with the Holy Spirit, and as the Holy Spirit pervades our lives—in every corner, every closet—he produces his fruit in us, primarily the love of God. All of this results in a growing capacity for love. The primary role of the Holy Spirit in our lives is to make real to our hearts the love and fatherhood of God (Rom. 8:14–15).

How, then, do we embrace God's love?

First of all we need to *comprehend his love.* Paul wrote, "And I pray that you, being rooted and established in love, may have power, together with all the Lord's people, to grasp how wide and long and high and deep is the love of Christ, and to know this love that surpasses knowledge—that you may be filled to the measure of all the fullness of God" (Eph. 3:17b–19). Paul said that to know God's love—just to get a better idea of how immense and amazing it is— would in and of itself be a transforming experience. If we could grasp the love of God in its full-blown dimensions, if we could grab hold of it for just a moment, we would understand something of all the fullness of God, because God is love.

Second, we need to *experience it*. Paul wrote, "Those who are led by the Spirit of God are the children of God. The Spirit you received does not make you slaves, so that you live in fear again; rather, the Spirit you received brought about your adoption to sonship. And by him we cry, 'Abba, Father'" (Rom. 8:14–15). Something in our hearts is so overwhelmed by love that it cannot help but call out in warmth and affection, "Daddy, I belong to you. You are my Daddy." We need to do more than understand his love in our minds. We need to allow it to move from our heads to our hearts. We need to learn to let God love us. We need to accept his love, to embrace it, to savor it. We must be convinced to the core of our being of his fatherly delight in us.

For years, the woundedness in my life made it difficult to receive a simple compliment or any affirmation. I could not believe I was lovable and found it easy simply to deflect affection as meaningless and irrelevant. We all have ways of blocking love at times, not letting it into our hearts. It is not an act of humility to reject love. We must learn to receive love from God and others. Ironically, a lot of prideful behavior grows out of insecurity. But when we are secure about our place in God's love we are set free to serve.

I talked recently with a bright and gifted twenty-three-year-old woman struggling with depression, bulimia, and cutting herself at times. My heart was pained by the story of many experiences that have damaged her heart, leaving her feeling so alone. She understood the basics of the Christian faith but found it difficult to believe that God loved her. But it's the very thing she must risk believing if she ever hopes to find healing. God watches in agony and longs for us to open our hearts to him.

How can we learn to savor God's love? His love may come to you in many ways: through worship, through reading or hearing a phrase of Scripture that speaks to your heart about his personal care, through drinking in the beauty of creation, through a touch of kindness from someone else, through an answered prayer. Whenever we encounter his love and goodness, we need to choose to stay connected to it—taking the time to contemplate its meaning, hold it in our hearts, allow ourselves to feel something about it, and remember it ... perhaps by describing it in a journal.

Love can't be compelled by the will of another person or created by self-discipline. C. S. Lewis described the human heart as a garden, with love as its fairest flower and "the will" as a tool to cultivate it. You are the gardener. But can you as a gardener make love grow? "Without life springing from the earth, without rain, light and heat descending from the sky, he could do nothing ... And unless his grace comes down, like the rain and the sunshine, we shall use this tool [our will] to very little purpose."[3] The capacity to love is a gift of God and it is best cultivated by the action of his love upon us. Invite God to love you. And as you experience his love, embrace it.

## —Making Love Real—

Spend some quiet time alone with God today. Let God love you. Read Ephesians 3:14–21. Ask God to open your heart to understand the magnitude of his love. Identify some of the ways God has revealed his love to you. Practice savoring God's love. Allow all of the blessings and positive feelings associated with his love to seep into your heart. Meditate on his love for all people (John 3:16–17; 2 Peter 3:9). Write your thoughts and feelings about your experience of his love.

❧

# Part Two

# What Does Love Look Like?

*If I speak with the eloquence of men and of angels, but have no love, I become no more than blaring brass or crashing cymbal. If I have the gift of foretelling the future and hold in my mind not only all human knowledge but the very secrets of God, and if I also have that absolute faith which can move mountains, but have no love, I amount to nothing at all. If I dispose of all that I possess, yes, even if I give my own body to be burned, but have no love, I achieve precisely nothing.*

*This love of which I speak is slow to lose patience — it looks for a way of being constructive. It is not possessive: it is neither anxious to impress nor does it cherish inflated ideas of its own importance.*

*Love has good manners and does not pursue selfish advantage. It is not touchy. It does not keep account of evil or gloat over the wickedness of other people. On the contrary, it shares the joy of those who live by the truth.*

*Love knows no limit to its endurance, no end to its trust, no fading of its hope; it can outlast anything. Love never fails.*

1 Corinthians 13:1–8 (ph)

*Love must be sincere. Hate what is evil; cling to what is good. Be devoted to one another in love. Honor one another above yourselves. Never be lacking in zeal, but keep your spiritual fervor, serving the Lord. Be joyful in hope, patient in affliction, faithful in prayer. Share with the Lord's people who are in need. Practice hospitality.*

*Bless those who persecute you; bless and do not curse. Rejoice with those who rejoice; mourn with those who mourn. Live in harmony with one another. Do not be proud, but be willing to associate with people of low position. Do not think you are superior.*

*Do not repay anyone evil for evil. Be careful to do what is right in the eyes of everyone. If it is possible, as far as it depends on you, live at peace with everyone. Do not take revenge, my dear friends, but leave room for God's wrath, for it is written: "It is mine to avenge; I will repay," says the Lord. On the contrary:*

*"If your enemy is hungry, feed him;*

*if he is thirsty, give him something to drink.*

*In doing this, you will heap burning coals on his head."*

*Do not be overcome by evil, but overcome evil with good.*

ROMANS 12:9–21

# 6

# An Adequate Foundation: Commitment

A crucial step in moving toward a more loving heart is having a sound understanding of what love is. But few of us can easily describe what we mean when we use the word *love*.

We throw the word *love* around, using it to describe an assortment of feelings and behaviors. Some of the abuse of the word is quite unintentional and relates to the limitations of the English language. We love our spouses. We love baseball. We love chocolate chip cookies. The word cannot mean the same thing in each case. We need to ask ourselves, what is love? What does a ripened and mature love look like? When we come upon the real article, how will we recognize it?

Many things described as love actually have nothing to

do with love at all. Parents who fail to discipline their child appropriately—or, conversely, who are overly controlling—may offer the excuse that they love the child too much. But such behavior, on either extreme, is not love at all. Love, as we're going to see, acts in the best interest of the beloved, and to fail to offer children the direction and discipline necessary to the formation of their character and their long-term well-being simply is not love. Likewise, when a parent is overcontrolling that is not love either, and in most cases has more to do with the parents' fear or comfort than with the child's well-being.

I have heard obsession described as loving too much. Obsession is not love; it has nothing at all to do with love. A man who acts inappropriately towards a married woman—using as his excuse the urgency of his feelings, saying that he is "in love"—is deluding himself. No matter how strong his feelings, his problem in that moment is not that he loves too much, but that he loves too little. If he truly loved her as God loves her, he would act in her best interest and would do nothing that would risk harm to her, her marriage, or her family. C. S. Lewis reminds us that if we love as God loves, we can never love another person too much. "We may love him too much *in proportion* to our love for God; but it is the smallness of our love for God, not the greatness of our love for the man, that constitutes the inordinacy."[1]

Some basic ideas about love emerge from the study of Scripture that give shape to this section of the book— hallmarks of love consistently emphasized throughout the Bible. In fact, the New Testament uses several specific

Greek words to describe various kinds of love. Our purpose here is not to draw distinctions between these various words for love but to grasp more fully God's love, *agape*, the pure and complete love to which God invites us. God's love is a very different kind of love from human love. Let me offer a practical definition of God's kind of love as it works itself out in human lives: *Love is a commitment of the will and a joy of the spirit that expresses itself in the choice to act in the best interest of the beloved.*

This definition has three parts, each of which is essential. First of all, to understand the love of God, we must first understand that God's love is rooted in commitment. His love expressed through a human life is characterized by the same kind of patience and faithfulness that he shows to us. Its limits are not dictated by emotions. We walk into a new relationship, bright eyed with a sense of awe and wonder about the other person, but then we find that he or she also struggles at life. This other person isn't as perfect as we first hoped; he or she, too, has problems. The relationship becomes more costly and difficult than we anticipated. *Agape* is a love that persists when the going gets tough, when it's not easy to love.

To say that love is a commitment of the will does not mean it's void of emotion. For love is also a joy of the spirit. There's a gladness, a goodness, a gleefulness to love. Loving is something we want to do much of the time because of the value we place on the beloved. Love is a dance between commitment and joy.

These foundational aspects of love consistently lead us to choose to act in the best interest of those we love.

Love is practical. It makes the choice to serve. Taken together these three ideas form a basic working definition of godly love that allows us to discuss more meaningfully the question of what love looks like.

# The Foundation of Godly Love

Commitment is foundational to an adequate understanding of God's love, *agape*. Paul emphasized commitment in his definition of love in 1 Corinthians 13. Love "always protects, always trusts, always hopes, always perseveres. Love never fails" (1 Cor. 13:7–8). J. B. Phillips translated this passage, "Love knows no limit to its endurance, no end to its trust, no fading of its hope; it can outlast anything." The bottom line in this biblical definition of love is commitment. Love is not fickle; it is not mere sentimentality; it's not subjective; it's more than a nice feeling. Love is concrete and practical because it is rooted and grounded in the character of God. God is love. When we talk about genuine love we must always realize that we're talking about what God is like. God's love is a love that never gives up on us. The Old Testament word for God's love requires more than one English word to convey its meaning—it is covenant-love, committed-love, faithful-love.

When Jesus wanted to reveal his Father's heart toward sinners, he told a story about a son who ran away from home, squandered the family's wealth, and dishonored his father. The portrayal of God as a father who waits, day after day, night after night, watching from the window, looking out with longing, desiring his son to come home—this is a picture of the loyalty and fidelity of God's love.[2] And when that son finally did come home, his father's love was still intact. The father's love never depended on the behavior of the son. It was always about who the father was. This is the nature of God's love for us. He never gives up on us—in fact, such relentless commitment is the hallmark of his love, and the foundation of all such committed loves we experience in life. The "no matter what" commitment of Christ to the church anticipates the commitment of marriage, and the "no matter what" commitment of our heavenly Father to each of us, his children, models the commitment of a parent to a child.

## Commitment and Community

Commitment has ramifications for community. M. Scott Peck argues that what one usually experiences in groups of people who are new to each other is what he calls "pseudo-community," a way of relating predicated on the denial of our individuality and differences of opinion. Everyone tries to get along, pretending that we all think the same and have the same values and opinions. Moving beyond pseudo-community to true community involves the pain of "chaos" and confusion that comes from being honest with each other about who we are and what we really think and feel. Because this process is painful we will tend to resist it. But we cannot move to a deeper level in our relationships without a willingness to endure the tunnel of confusion, hanging in there, and seeing our way through to the other end.[3]

In the midst of "chaos," the worst manifestations of our tendency toward competition and comparison emerge. We want to prove ourselves right, or better, or more worthy of praise than the person next to us. Only through committed love can we choose to patiently remain with each other and endure the pain of conflict until we reach the deeper places of understanding and acceptance awaiting us on the other side of the chaos.

In my early college days I had the privilege of being mentored briefly by a quiet, unassuming man named Mel Friesen. Mel suffered with interstitial lung disease. He lost one lung. He had ongoing pain from collapsed vertebrae caused by the steroids necessary to control his lung disease. In spite of the emotional effects of steroid use and severe pain, he continued to live with great patience, kindness, and careful attention to the needs of others. His wife, Helen, shared with me after his death that at one of his regular visits his doctor told her that Mel had good reason for anger and irritability with his pain, illness, and the effects of the medication. He encouraged her to let him know that it was okay if he needed to let loose and be a little angry and irritable. Mel's response to Helen as she explained the doctor's concern later that day was, "Jesus didn't ask me to be kind only when I felt like it." This attitude was typical of Mel, who placed the highest possible value on the call of Jesus. Often, whether or not we love well comes down to simple choice.

## Commitment and Marriage

Dietrich Bonhoeffer, the great German pastor and theologian, was imprisoned for his opposition to the Nazis and his involvement in a plot to assassinate Hitler. He remained in prison until he was hanged days before the end of World War II. He wrote many letters that were later compiled in a book. One of these messages was to his nephew, written on the eve of his wedding. "A Wedding Sermon from a Prison Cell" contains an amazing statement about the nature of married love:

> In your love you see only the heaven of your own happiness, but in marriage you are placed at a post of responsibility towards the world and mankind. Your love is your own private possession, but marriage is more than something personal—it is a status, an office. Just as it is the crown, and not merely the will to rule, that makes the king, so it is marriage, and not merely your love for each other, that joins you together in the sight of God and man.... *It is not your love that sustains the marriage, but from now on, the marriage that sustains your love.*[4]

Bonhoeffer understood that love is ultimately about commitment. It's not the warm feelings that sustain the relationship; it's the ongoing choice we make to stay together through thick and thin.

Jacob's love for Rachel is described in what I consider the most romantic verse in the Bible. "So Jacob served seven years to get Rachel, but they seemed like only a few days to him because of his love for her" (Gen. 29:20). That's God's kind of love—joy and passion mixed with commitment and hard work.

The best definition of married love I've ever read came from a woman who had been married for twenty-seven years and had raised six children with her husband. She once said that "love is what you've been through with somebody."[5] Love isn't meant to last only a few months or years, then fade away. It is meant for a lifetime. Love becomes more fully itself only in the long haul. And commitment is the glue that holds our lives together and causes us to stay the course.

We have all seen marriages fail. We have witnessed choices to betray and abandon that have dealt mortal wounds to relationships where love once ruled. Hardness of heart and selfish choices lead to circumstances where even God allows divorce (Matt. 19:1–12). We have also witnessed relationships that have died slow and quiet deaths from passive neglect.

Perhaps you're in a marriage that's going through a hard time right now. You've experienced a number of rough spots and things don't seem to get better. Without ignoring the steps you may need to take to address the challenges you face in your relationship, I encourage you to see that it will be worth it to endure. The goodness, the blessing, the richness of love is something you dis-cover over the long haul.

Even in the best marriages there are days when you get up and you don't like each other very much. All mar-riages experience a kind of ebb and flow of emotions, passion, sexual intimacy, frustration. But God asks us to continue to love each other and to make the choice to be there for each other. The ability to go through diffi-cult times—to hit those rough spots but still remain committed and work for resolution, for intimacy—can lead to real joy and the depths of love. To give up with-out the hard work of living out your commitment is to miss the opportunity of a lifetime and reject one of your best chances to grow in knowledge of God's love.

I'm not saying that the problems are irrelevant. I'm not saying we don't need help along the way. I'm not try-ing to argue that God never allows divorce. But in our struggles we may need to do more than passively endure. We need to give our spouses and our marriages the hard work, energy, and attention they deserve. Marriage works because we are committed to each other, and sometimes commitment comes down to hard work.

## The Alternative to Commitment

The alternative to this kind of commitment in love is the emotional milieu that drives so much of our culture today. When God is displaced from his rightful place in the human soul, other gods are waiting to move in. Often the most convenient substitute is simply ourselves. First published about twenty-five years ago, *Psychology As Religion: The Cult of Self-Worship* by Paul Vitz is one of the most important books I've read describing the spirit of our age. Vitz writes that the religion of our day is "self-ism": the measure of the universe is the world as it affects me. Though psychological insight can provide tremendous benefit, without a proper context it can be detrimental and add to our confusion. Vitz argues that for many, "psychology has become a religion, in particular, a form of secular humanism based on worship of the self."[6]

What does this mean for relationships? Well, it means that as long as a relationship is serving my interests, keeping me happy and entertained, then I'll stick with it. But when that relationship no longer satisfies my needs and makes me happy, then I'm going to get rid of it, because I'm the center of my universe. For many this is the religion of the day. Its consequences are devastating. Vitz writes:

> For selfists there seem to be no acceptable duties, denials, inhibitions, or restraints. Instead, there are only rights and opportunities for change. An overwhelming number of the selfists assume that there are no unvarying moral or interpersonal relationships, no permanent aspects to individuals. All is written in sand by a self in flux.[7]

The great need of the day is for people who are willing to offer love that can be counted on—that is, the very love of God. Such committed love provides the security and stability that helps us become the individuals God wants us to be. This kind of love has the power to remove our defensiveness and to move us toward relationships of warmth and intimacy.

# An Example of Commitment

The prophet Hosea married a woman because God told him to. We don't even know what the prophet felt about her. She was a wild woman, described as "promiscuous," but he obeyed God and married her. She gave birth to a son. And God told the prophet Hosea to name his son Jezreel, because that name would always remind him of a place of terrible desolation in the past history of Israel. What a negative thing to name your son! Then a year later they had a daughter, and God told the prophet to name her Lo-Ruhammah, which means "one who has not received mercy." Hosea must have been shocked again, wondering why he should name his daughter such a thing. But as the kids got older, he looked at them and realized that they didn't look much like him. He had a third child, and his name was Lo-Ammi, which means "not my people." Suddenly the message became clear. Hosea was raising three illegitimate children. Not only was he raising them, but Gomer, his wife, was coming home less often. She was staying away all night most of the time. Hosea had become a virtual single parent, running the house, loving and caring for the children.

Eventually, Gomer moved out of the house and started working as a temple prostitute to the Baals and actually ended up in slavery to a pimp.

How do you think the great, godly Hosea felt about married life at this point? His life was filled with pain—infidelity, shame, anger, betrayal, and abandonment.

One day God said to Hosea, "Hosea, my people Israel have always been like that. They go to church and bring their offerings and sing worship songs, and then they go and chase after other gods, and I feel exactly what you feel. But, Hosea, I want you to understand something about my love. It's not a love that gives up on people. I want you to take everything that you own and pack it on your donkey, and I want you to hock it all and take the money and buy Gomer out of slavery, and I want you to bring her home. I want you to love her and teach her and help her to live a godly life."

So here's the great prophet of God, loved by the nation. Before the whole city, in public view, he packed up everything he owned—all of the silver, all of the dishes, all the utensils, all the appliances, all the jewelry—packed it up on his donkey. He walked down to the town, to the local pawn shop, sold everything that he had, took a handful of money, then went down the street to deal with some pimp and bought his wife back out of slavery.

There she was: naked, emaciated, diseased, no longer the desire of anybody. Hosea bought her back. He covered her up, placed her on his donkey, took her home, nursed her, fed her, brought her back to health. He restored her, forgave her, loved her, and began teaching her the Scripture and schooling her in righteousness.

Go back to that house fifteen years later and you find the couple truly in love with each other. Jezreel, now a strapping young man, is confident, loving the Lord, part of an intact family. Hosea has become more of a man than he ever was before, able to say to the Lord, "Now I understand to the depths of my being how deeply God loves sinners and how deliberately he keeps them and saves them."

Just think for a moment of Hosea, his humility, his service, his sacrifice. Think of the way he trusted God. Think of his commitment to God and to his wife. Consider the power and integrity of his words as he prophesies to the nation on behalf of God:

> I will betroth you to me forever; I will betroth you in right-eousness and justice, in love and compassion.
>
> I will betroth you in faithfulness, and you will acknowl-edge the LORD.... I will plant her for myself in the land; I will show my love to the one I called "Not my loved one."
>
> I will say to those called "Not my people," "You are my people"; and they will say, "You are my God." (Hos. 2:19–20, 23)

## It All Comes Down to Choice

The commitment to love is both a superdecision—an overarching decision about the way we will live—as well as a choice we make moment by moment. As Paul said to the Philippians in the face of persecution and possible death, "Whatever happens, as citizens of heaven live in a manner worthy of the gospel of Christ" (Phil. 1:27). Problems and struggles are not an excuse for poor behavior and giving up your commitment to love. Rather, when times are tough, remember the faithfulness of God's love, and the work of the Holy Spirit in making his love real to our hearts. Regardless of what happens, choose love.

# —Making Love Real—

As your Father, God will never give up on you. Nothing can ever separate you from him and his love for you. Identify a relationship with a family member or a close friend in which there have been some setbacks, where forgiveness has been difficult, and where reconciliation is needed. As you pray for your relationship, ask God to show you what loving that person with God's committed love might lead you to do. What steps do you need to take? What's stopping you from beginning that process today?

# 7

# Making Others Important: Humility

Our natural tendency, because of the damage sin has done to our souls, is to be preoccupied with our needs, our wants, our own happiness. That's a tidy theological statement. The truth is far worse. Most of the time my mind is filled with endless thoughts of myself, concerns for myself, desires for myself. It is like a car radio that only receives one station. It's all about me. Other voices emerge asking for my attention for a while, but when they are gone life is all about me once again. I have to admit that I don't usually feel guilty about this aspect of my condition. Because I've done it so long, it's hard to realize that I'm doing it and that there is any other way to live.

Being married and having children has helped. I now

have more moments than I used to when I am genuinely concerned about someone else. But even when I'm concerned about someone else it can somehow be about me and how things affect me.

It's even worse when I'm going through a difficult time. When I am insecure, fearful, when my life seems out of control, someone has to take care of me; and most of the time I think the best person for the job is me. It goes without saying that when life is all about me my capacity for love is stunted.

Love is characterized by humility. Paul wrote, "Do nothing out of selfish ambition or vain conceit. Rather, in humility value others above yourselves, not looking to your own interests but each of you to the interests of the others" (Phil. 2:3–4). Elsewhere he wrote, "Be devoted to one another in love. Honor one another above yourselves" (Rom. 12:10). He described love as "not self-seeking" (1 Cor. 13:5). Humility involves the ability to lift our eyes off of our own needs and to see someone else's needs, to be fully present in the moment, to care for someone else. But how do we stop our continual preoccupation with ourselves?

The choice to consider other people as more important than ourselves is contrary to everything we experience in this world. Where in our education are we taught that it is healthy to think of others as more important than ourselves? Only God shows us the way of love in the example of Jesus, who though he is Lord and Creator chooses to empty himself and die because of his loving concern for our well-being.

## An Example of Humility

Jesus provided a powerful example of the humility of love. For three years Jesus carefully did everything the Father asked him to do. He systematically laid out a comprehensive body of teaching about life in the kingdom of God. Even in his final hours he still reached out to the disciples, trying to help them understand what was most important about his life and love. Everything he lived for depended on whether or not the disciples learned how to have deep, authentic, lasting relationships. Everything he worked for hinged on their ability to love one another deeply from the heart, and to recognize that they were indeed a family. In his final moments he endeavored one last time to help them understand (John 13:1–17).

People in Jesus' day traveled on foot, barefoot, or with open shoes, and their feet were dirty and smelly by the time they got to their destination. In homes where there was enough money servants had differing levels of responsibility, and it was the job of the lowest servant in the house to wash the dirty feet of anyone who visited the home.

The disciples had secured a room for the Last Supper. As they arrived, they realized there was no servant in this borrowed room to wash their feet. Each disciple apparently said to himself, "Hey, no one's going to wash our feet. We'll wait until one of the lesser disciples gets here." But all of them made the same decision. "I'm not the lowest person in the house. I'm not about to wash anyone's feet." The dirt on their feet became a witness to their pride. None of them was up to the job of washing the others' feet. Pride destroys our capacity to love by convincing our hearts that we must come out on top and be honored above another.

Not only did the disciples refuse to be servants by washing each other's feet, we're told in Luke that during supper the disciples argued with one another about which of them was considered the greatest (Luke 22:24). Clearly, they were unprepared to be servants.

Imagine how outlandish it was to the disciples, then, to see Jesus take a basin of water and strip down to his undergarment and assume the role of the lowest servant. It was so shocking that Peter's response seems justified; he initially refused to let Jesus wash his feet. Through this simple but profound act of humility, Jesus showed the disciples what it meant to honor others above yourself. It means we take the attention and the recognition we believe to be ours and give it to someone else. We take our need to be in the limelight and step back and allow others to stand in that light. It means that we choose to use the position and the power God has given us to serve others.

Jesus turned to the disciples and challenged them. *Do you understand what I have done for you? I have used my position and power to serve you; I have honored you above myself. Now this is to be the pattern of relationships among those who follow me.* "Now that I, your Lord and Teacher, have washed your feet, you also should wash one another's feet" (John 13:12–14). This is not an example to be told as a story. This is something you are to do. This is an example to be lived out. "Very truly I tell you, servants are not greater than their master, nor are messengers greater than the one who sent them" (John 13:16).

Nothing challenges our pride like serving. When we become a servant to someone else, our feelings about that person change as a sense of mutual belonging emerges, our hearts change as the dysfunctional aspects of our appetites and self-absorption are challenged. We acknowledge with our bodies and actions that life is not about us.

## Humility Involves Valuing Others

The gospel writers consistently express two aspects of Jesus' response to those who come to him for help. First, *Jesus never met a human being he was not willing to serve.* The way Jesus responded to women and children; his care for non-Jews such as the Samaritan woman, the Syrophoenician woman, the Roman centurion; his love for tax collectors like Zacchaeus and Matthew; and his grace to the woman caught in adultery, the man lowered through the roof, and the man born blind all demonstrate his capacity to see beyond the culturally defined determination of a person's value and to see the tattered image of God within each person. C. S. Lewis wrote:

The load, or weight, or burden of my neighbour's glory should be laid on my back, a load so heavy that only humility can carry it, and the backs of the proud will be broken. It is a serious thing to live in a society of possible gods and goddesses, to remember that the dullest and most uninteresting person you can talk to may one day be a creature which, if you saw it now, you would be strongly tempted to worship, or else a horror and a corruption such as you now meet, if at all, only in a nightmare.... There are no *ordinary* people. You have never talked to a mere mortal.... But it is immortals whom we joke with, work with, marry, snub, and exploit—immortal horrors or everlasting splendours.... Next to the Blessed Sacrament itself, your neighbour is the holiest object presented to your senses.[1]

The second principle that emerges from Christ's example is this: Anytime someone came to Jesus for help *the grace he gave was always greater than the grace that was sought.* Jesus always goes the second mile. The first specific miracle of Jesus recorded in Mark's gospel was the healing of a man with leprosy (Mark 1:40–45). This man, perhaps forty years old, likely had not been touched by physical kindness from another human being for decades because he was ceremonially unclean. This man came to Jesus and said, "If you are willing, you can make me clean." Jesus touched this man and said, "I am willing. Be clean!" We know that Jesus often healed without touch. He could simply have spoken the words at a distance. But this man needed the touch of another person. When Jesus embraced that man, he was every bit a leper. When Jesus released that man, he was clean. I can easily imagine that this man had probably given up the idea that God heard his cries for help. But Jesus touched him, and perhaps for the first time in his life he knew that there was a God in heaven who cared about him. The man sought physical healing, but Jesus gave him much more—healing that was physical, emotional, and spiritual.

How do we account for the changes in the Samaritan woman in the course of Jesus' encounter with her in John 4? First of all, Jesus relates to her in such a way that she feels valued and significant. She leaves her water jar at the well, runs back to the town, and shares her good news. "Come, see a man who told me everything I ever did. Could this be the Messiah?" *He knows me as I really am and he cares about me. He is unlike anyone I have ever known.* She is transformed— the outcast has become the messenger, her sense of shame displaced by significance.

Jesus also offers her the possibility of a different life. "Those who drink the water I give them will never thirst. Indeed, the water I give them will become in them a spring of water welling up to eternal life." A woman of reputation racked by the pain and isolation of her own choices becomes the town evangelist exert- ing tremendous influence in her joy and transformation as Jesus answers the deepest longings of her heart. We are told that "many of the Samaritans from that town believed in him because of the woman's testimony, 'He told me everything I ever did.'" The grace that Jesus gave was always greater than the grace that was sought.

# Humility Involves Letting Go of the Need to Be Important

We all have an idea of how human relationships are supposed to work. For most of us these ideas include some system of hierarchy. In such a structure the goal of each relationship is to gain enough influence, power, and control to get other people to do what you want them to. Jesus does not reject altogether the idea of some type of hierarchy within relationships. What Jesus does argue is that people in higher positions, people with more power and influence, are to choose to become servants to those with less. "You know that those who are regarded as rulers of the Gentiles lord it over them, and their high officials exercise authority over them. Not so with you. Instead, whoever wants to become great among you must be your servant, and whoever wants to be first must be slave of all" (Mark 10:42–44).

I have to ponder how difficult this choice really is. We come to the place in our lives where we are finally on top, in charge, and Jesus tells us to drop it all and choose to live in the kingdom of God by becoming a servant. We face a real choice at this point.

John wrote, "Jesus knew that the Father had put all things under his power, and that he had come from God and was returning to God" (John 13:3). The fundamental questions of life and destiny were settled for Jesus. He knew who he was. He knew what God's plan was. He knew where he had come from. He knew where he was going. He knew he was loved.

When we are insecure we have a lot to prove, don't we? We struggle with the need to establish ourselves as important, especially when the fundamental question of who we are has not been sufficiently answered. But when we are secure, we are set free to love and to serve. We understand that what others think and say about us really doesn't matter.

Paul described Jesus' attitude this way: "Who, being in very nature God, did not consider equality with God something to be used to his own advantage; rather, he made himself nothing" (Phil. 2:6–7). Picture for a moment the outer reaches of heaven filled with the glory of God. Imagine the triune God enthroned in space, radiant in holiness and glory, with innumerable angels encompassing him, calling out, "Holy, holy, holy is the Lord Almighty." And in the midst of this unimaginable glory we find unbelievable humility—humility that allows the preexistent Word to say, "I will go; I will leave this place of authority, and I will honor those people above myself." Because Jesus loves us he accepted birth in a stable, chose a life of sorrow, insults, and grief, knowing he would one day hang naked upon a cross as a condemned criminal. By his example he makes one thing clear—God is the most humble being in the universe. The proof of God's love and humility is that he places us above himself.

God invites us to a lifetime of humility and service. It's worth repeating that Paul wrote, "Do nothing out of selfish ambition or vain conceit. Rather, in humility value others above yourselves, not looking to your own interests but each of you to the interests of the others" (Phil. 2:3–4). "Live in harmony with one another. Do not be proud, but be willing to associate with people of low position. Do not think you are superior" (Rom. 12:16).

Humility means setting aside self for the good of others. Recently I attended a high school graduation where the president of a secular university asked the graduates to evaluate their attitudes on some important questions. Among other things he asked them how they felt about children. He argued rather effectively that in recent decades we have experienced tremendous gains as adults in rights, privileges, and freedoms. And we have used these freedoms to pursue a course of self-fulfillment and self-actualization that is often carried out to the detriment of children who need our time, attention, and affection. He stated that it is time for adults to set aside some of our rights and privileges in order to focus on the rights and needs of children. It had been quite some time since I had heard someone in the public arena call on others to set aside their privileges to serve others.

# The Joy of Humility

Real happiness comes in serving others. Remember how Jesus ends his teaching: "Now that you know these things, *you will be blessed if you do them*" (John 13:17). Parents want their children to succeed. They are happiest when their children are doing well. That is the sort of love Jesus wants us all to have for each other. We can't be afraid that to give away a slice of the approval pie for fear that it will somehow rob us of our own glory. One of the acid tests of genuine love in our relationships is the ability to honor others above ourselves by enjoying and celebrating their successes and accomplishments above our own.

When I had no relationship with my father, men in the church loved me as a son. Before I was ever married I had families that accepted me as a member. Before I had children, I had children who depended on me as a parent. David described God as "a father to the fatherless, a defender of widows" who "sets the lonely in families" (Ps. 68:5–6). We are all mothers and fathers in the kingdom of God, whether or not we are married, whether we are biological parents or adoptive parents. We are family. As Paul wrote, "Do not think of yourself more highly than you ought.... In Christ we, though many, form one body, and each member belongs to all the others" (Rom. 12:3, 5). At the end of his book *The Wounded Healer* Henri Nouwen writes: "We do not know where we will be two, ten or twenty years from now. What we can know, however, is that man suffers and that a sharing of suffering can make us move forward."[2]

When Caitlin, our daughter, was six months old she had a difficult surgery involving her mouth and airway. Afterward her arms were splinted to keep her from pulling at her IV and touching the surgical site. The recovery was long and uncomfortable for her. For three days and nights she was in the hospital. Carole would not leave her side. For seventy-two hours Carole went without adequate food, a comfortable place to sleep, and a shower. She did it gladly. As a physician I have watched dozens if not hundreds of parents sacrifice all comforts and resources to care for their children. Something about the way we love our children causes us to put their needs before our own. This is humility, one of the hallmarks of genuine love. It involves a healthy self-forgetfulness. Jesus invites us to this kind of love in our relationships with each other.

## —Making Love Real—

Choosing to serve has a profound effect upon our hearts by helping us connect with other people and challenging our tendency toward self-absorption. When we serve, we acknowledge with our bodies and actions that life is not about us.

Search for an opportunity to be a servant to somebody this week. It doesn't need to be anything big or glamorous (though it certainly could be!)—just a way to meet a real need in somebody else's life. For example, rake the leaves off of an elderly neighbor's yard, read to someone at a convalescent hospital, prepare a package of good food for a homeless person, or bake something for a neighbor you've never connected with. As you serve, open your eyes to what God sees in the people you serve.

# 8

# Using Our Power for Others: Gentleness

I did not anticipate the magnitude of my emotions when, at the moment of Jonathan's birth, I sobbed with overwhelming joy and gratitude. Moments later I held him for the first time. I remember the keen sense of how tiny and fragile he was. Eight pounds, two ounces.

As we took him home from the hospital you would have thought I had never driven before. We fastened the car seat securely and then drove home—at about fifteen miles per hour. At every intersection I would look back and forth over and over again, hesitant to go no matter how far I could see. I kept asking myself what in the world I was doing. I was driving like an idiot. I was aware of the precious little life in the back seat, so fragile, so helpless, and I wanted to do everything I could to protect him.

When I think of the feelings of care I experience as a parent I am reminded of God's care for us. Is he any less tender toward us? Is he any less concerned about our frailty?

## The Gentleness of God

Sometimes I act or speak with little awareness of the consequence of my words and actions. But the God who speaks into existence a universe beyond our comprehension moves through this world with such care and gentleness that most of the time we don't even know he's here. The philosopher and pastor Søren Kierkegaard wrote, "He is God; and yet he has not a resting place for his head ... He is God; and yet he picks his steps more carefully than if angels guided them, not to prevent his foot from stumbling against a stone, but lest he trample human beings in the dust, in that they are offended at him. He is God; and yet his eye surveys mankind with anxious care, for the tender shoots of an individual life may be crushed as easily as a blade of grass."[1]

When we look closely at Jesus we begin to understand this gentle aspect of God's character. On one occasion Jesus healed a man with a paralyzed, atrophied hand on the Sabbath. The Pharisees, angered by Jesus' repudiation of their heartless interpretation of the law and his claim to be "Lord of the Sabbath," began to plot how they were going to kill him. The story continues:

Aware of this, Jesus withdrew from that place. A large crowd followed him, and he healed all who were ill. He warned them not to tell others about him. This was to fulfill what was spoken through the prophet Isaiah:

"Here is my servant whom I have chosen, the one I love, in whom I delight; I will put my Spirit on him, and he will proclaim justice to the nations. He will not quarrel or cry out; no one will hear his voice in the streets. A bruised reed he will not break, and a smoldering wick he will not snuff out, till he leads justice to victory. In his name the nations will put their hope." (Matt. 12:15–21)

Matthew saw the fulfillment of Isaiah's prophecy in the way Jesus strictly forbade those he healed to tell anyone about it. He wasn't interested in media hype.

## Gentleness Begins in the Restraint of Power

The first thing we learn from Jesus' example is that *gentleness involves the restraint of power*. Jesus is the anticipated champion of justice for an oppressed and demoralized people, according to Isaiah. He has power and influence at his disposal beyond our wildest imagination, yet he refuses to accomplish his mission by means of the things that we associate with power. Instead, Jesus is a servant who sets his power aside.

We compete and debate, seeking to overwhelm each other with the strength of our arguments, and making sure everyone knows that we have something worth saying. But when Jesus comes to us today—just as he did in the Gospels—he does not quarrel or raise his voice.

If our message does not sell itself, we'll find a way to sell it. We brighten it, embellish it, put it on bumpers, billboards, and television. We hire the energetic and attractive to push it to the masses. But Jesus does not shout or allow his voice to be heard in the streets.

We train for assertiveness, search for ways to improve ourselves, to become more powerful and appealing. But Jesus refuses to overpower even the weakest and most bruised among us.

Though the broken and the weak appear to be of little use, the actions of Jesus consistently contradict this harsh law of the world. The disciples were good enough businessmen to know that the kingdom of God could not be built on the shoulders of women and children, prostitutes, tax collectors, and "sinners." But those were the very people for whom the gentleness of God had the greatest appeal.

Have you ever felt like a smoldering wick—so frail that anyone but the gentlest person would just snuff you out? In some periods of my life I have felt that weak. But Jesus met me there. His power could have easily snuffed me out; but he didn't. Instead, he came to me in gentleness.

I mentioned earlier my friend and mentor in college Mel Friesen. Mel and his wife, Helen, are legends of InterVarsity Christian Fellowship on the West Coast and two of the finest people I have ever known. They're known for their unyielding determination to following Jesus no matter the cost. I first met Mel at a college retreat where he was teaching. Helen also taught a seminar on hospitality that weekend. She told us about an encounter they had when they were first married and involved in campus ministry with InterVarsity at UCLA back in the early '50s. One day on their way home from work they walked past a man who obviously had been living on the streets for a long time. Mel invited him home to dinner. At their apartment Mel talked to this man at the table while Helen prepared the best meal she could. They sat down to eat, and it immediately became apparent that this man didn't know how to eat with a knife and fork. He picked up his knife and began to eat his meal with just his knife. Helen said she felt a little uncomfortable and wasn't quite sure what to do. So she looked at Mel. She said that Mel, without a pause or added twinge of expression, picked up his knife and proceeded to eat his entire meal with just his knife. He didn't have to think about what to do. When I heard that story, and when I think of it again now, I see it as a picture of the gentleness of God worked out in a human life.

As difficult as it may be for us to understand, it was in the restraint of his power, the laying aside of his power, that Jesus fulfilled his mission on earth.

## Gentleness Reveals the Power of God

About twenty years ago I had my gall bladder out. I had several episodes of terrible pain, and it was time to have it out. This happened before the advent of laparoscopy. The procedure was major surgery, and I was in the hospital a couple of days afterward. As I was recovering from surgery and feeling a bit miserable, an older man who had just come from surgery was brought into the room to the other bed. He had previously had surgery to remove a cancer from his nose. That day they had taken a big flap of skin from his forehead and reconstructed his nose. So he had two wounds and was obviously suffering a lot of pain.

He was a gracious man, easy to talk with. He was Jewish. I thought of engaging him in a discussion about spiritual matters but couldn't bring myself to talk to him about anything challenging or stimulating because he seemed so miserable. On the second day some friends from the seminary I attended came to visit. Don Heckman came with his son, Stephen, who was five years old. When they were ready to leave Don said to Stephen, "Let's pray for Uncle Phil." Stephen quietly prayed a beautiful prayer, asking God for my healing and to be with me. My roommate carefully observed the visit with great curiosity. A few minutes after they left, he began to ask some questions about the Heckmans. He wanted to know who they were, what they did, if they went to church. Finally he said, "You know, I couldn't believe that little boy's prayer. He just talked to God so person-ally, so sincerely, as if he really knew him. I don't think I've ever heard anyone pray like that. It really was very special. It makes me think about my own relationship with God. I don't think I know him like that little boy." This opened the door for us to share our hearts with each other. But the thing we kept coming back to was the faith of that five-year-old. It was the gentleness of God that won the day—not powerful words, not the big arguments.

I don't understand it. How can God's power be manifested in gentleness? This seems so backward. It seems upside down. But that's how life in the kingdom of God is, isn't it? The heart of the gospel is, as Jesus put it, that when the mighty Son of Man came to live among his creatures, he came not to lord it over them and to be served by them, but to serve them and to give his life as a ransom for many (Mark 10:45).

God's power is revealed in his gentleness. Ultimately the greatest demonstration of God's power was seen when God reached his mighty hand into human history and allowed it to be nailed to a cross. In the cross we find the proof of what others have written, that there is nothing as strong as gentleness and nothing so gentle as real strength.

## A Spirituality of Gentleness

It is his gentleness that affects the whole of my spirituality and every aspect of my walk with Jesus. When I am tempted to believe that the "success" of my walk with Jesus is wrapped up in personal accomplishment or other people's opinion of me, I remember the words of Isaiah regarding the Lord Jesus when he wrote, "He was despised and rejected by others, a man of suffering, and familiar with pain. Like one from whom people hide their faces he was despised, and we held him in low esteem" (Isa. 53:3). These days, there is plenty of material available to convince me that the goal of my walk with Jesus is to be dynamic, powerful, and useful, to always be on top of things, to look like a winner, to be a success. But then I'm reminded of Jesus' words, "Come to me, all you who are weary and burdened, and I will give you rest. Take my yoke upon you and learn from me, for I am gentle and humble in heart, and you will find rest for your souls. For my yoke is easy and my burden is light" (Matt. 11:28–30).

When I hear these words I remember my real condition—my brokenness, my dependence—and I experience a tremendous sense of relief. Who does he invite? He invites the dimly burning. He beckons the broken blades of grass. He calls out to frail, suffering, struggling people like us. Why should we come? What is his argument? He says we should come because of what he is like. "I am gentle and humble in heart."

In all four gospels this is the only place that Jesus described himself at the level of his character and personality. And what are the two words that Jesus used to describe himself? *Gentle* and *humble*. With these words he invites us. "If you are hurting and broken, you can come to me, you can trust me with your pain, because of what I am like."

Among religious people today the spirit of humility is all too often lost and replaced with a spirit of judgment and rigidity about the correctness of our thinking. We may encounter "loving" people who too easily overlook blatant sin in their own lives or in the lives of others and who, lacking strong convictions, are ambivalent about the truth. We may also encounter "righteous" people who see sin everywhere and point it out harshly, without humility or grace. The problem is that neither approach is particularly loving or particularly righteous; with one we deny people the badly needed truth, and with the other we deny them respect and communicate in a way that makes it all but impossible for them to hear. It is increasingly rare to find those who know how to "speak the truth in love" (Eph. 4:15).

Christians should be known for their capacity to care deeply and passionately about the truth and to convey their thoughts with love and humility. As Richard Mouw put it, "The real challenge is to come up with a *convicted civility*."[2] No matter how high our view of the authority of Scripture may be, we remain plagued by our own fallibility, knowledge that exceeds our character, and an inadequate capacity for love. These factors leave a great deal of room for humility in our discourse with and about people with whom we disagree. Civility is not optional for the follower of Jesus Christ, even when we believe we are right, because it is a manifestation of his humility and gentleness.

## Experiencing the Gentleness of God

In Hosea we find a powerful monologue where God expresses with dramatic shifts both his anger over Israel's sin and idolatry and his parental love and sense of mercy:

When Israel was a child, I loved him, and out of Egypt I called my son. But the more they were called, the more they went away from me. They sacrificed to the Baals and they burned incense to images. It was I who taught Ephraim to walk, taking them by the arms; but they did not realize it was I who healed them. I led them with cords of human kindness, with ties of love. To them I was like one who lifts a little child to the cheek, and I bent down to feed them.

Will they not return to Egypt and will not Assyria rule over them because they refuse to repent? Swords will flash in their cities, will destroy the bars of their gates and put an end to their plans. My people are determined to turn from me. Even though they call me God Most High, I will by no means exalt them.

How can I give you up, Ephraim? How can I hand you over, Israel? How can I treat you like Admah? How can I make you like Zeboyim? My heart is changed within me; all my compassion is aroused. I will not carry out my fierce anger, nor will I devastate Ephraim again. For I am God, and not a human being—the Holy One among you. I will not come against their cities. (Hos. 11:1–9)

It's as if God were saying, "If I treated you the way you treat each other, if I were as humble as you are, you'd all be dead. But I'm not like you. I restrain my power. I respond to you with kindness, compassion, gentleness. My parental care tempers my response to your constant disobedience."

Years ago while visiting family in Washington we stopped overnight at my sister's home in the outskirts of Olympia. We had just finished dinner and I was at the sink cleaning up when Carole called out that Brendan was choking. He was one year old at the time. He was already blue and in obvious distress. I attempted the Heimlich maneuver; I picked him up and smacked him in the back a couple of times. He seemed to be making a little sound so I set him down. But he was still choking, so I did it a second time. I tried to sweep his mouth, which you're not supposed to do, and that didn't do any good. I was desperate.

I picked him up and I looked into his face, and for the first time in his life I could tell he was unconscious. He was no longer responsive at all. I felt his life slipping away. And in that moment I experienced something more powerful than any fear I have ever felt, a feeling of pain and fear and desperation that cut through my entire being. I'm still affected by the memory of that feeling. I called out in my mind, "Lord, help me to know what to do."

I was a first-year medical student and knew just enough to know that I didn't know what I was doing and how desperate the situation was. I thought for a moment about what they would do in the emergency room. We had called 911 and had been on the line with the operator for about a minute. The paramedics were on their way. It would be five or ten minutes until they would get there because we were out in the country. I knew they would attempt to clear his airway. They would have the proper instruments to do that and I didn't have them. So I reached down the side of his mouth with my finger as far down his throat as I could, and I could tell right away that I had reached what was obstructing his airway. So I pulled out a squashed grape and a whole grape that was lodged in his airway. For a moment there was no response, and then he threw up and started breathing. He quickly recovered.

I was changed by what I experienced in that moment. For a while, of course, I was far more paranoid about potential choking hazards. I've always been a safety-first creature. For a while Brendan ate nothing larger than half a pea. But something else changed in me. The experience opened a small window of insight into the way God feels about us. Think about the pain I felt in that moment of crisis. Those intense feelings of pain and fear emanated from the tremendous value I place on Brendan. The extent of my pain was shaped by the depth of my love. God's love for us is infinitely greater than my love for Brendan. It is unfathomable.

Right now, wherever you are, whatever you're doing, whatever you're feeling, God is looking at you, passionately concerned about you. You have his undivided attention. Your past choices, the condition of your heart, the degree of your brokenness are no obstacle to relationship with him. Because he is gentle and humble he invites us to come to him. Every moment in the presence of God is an opportunity to have our eternal destiny shaped by what happens from this moment forward rather than by anything in our past. His grace is always greater than our ability to mess things up. The slightest exertion of his power or anger over sin would consume us. With exquisite tenderness he reaches out his hand to save us and to touch our lives in a way that will heal us and make us whole.

The kingdom of God may be enhanced and even built in some small part on powerful words and actions, but what will absolutely turn this world upside down—not by some irony but by design—is one word spoken in kindness, one tender touch offered in love, one cup of cold water given in the name of Jesus, one life, perhaps your life, made all over again by the gentleness of God.

# —Making Love Real—

Jesus' life on earth was a continuous act of gentleness. The God of righteousness, justice, and infinite power accepted the confines of our humanity, lived among us as our servant, died a brutal death in order to bear our sins, and then invited us to participate in his victory over sin and death.

So many of our experiences in life point to assertiveness and the use of whatever power we have as the best approach to getting what we want. It seems to me that part of the appeal of Jesus to broken people is his gentleness. They know they aren't going to get squashed or ignored by another person driven by self-interest.

Look for an opportunity to be gentle with others this week. Really look at the people you interact with, listen carefully, become "small," let them be the focus, express care, and seek to make their life better because you were there for them.

# 9

# Love Is Practical and Costly: Kindness

❧

Years ago I came across a story in the paper about twin brothers in Florida. One of the brothers wanted to donate one of his kidneys to his ailing brother who had complete kidney failure—one kidney had been removed soon after his birth and the other had failed. The parents and others had tried to donate. No compatible donor could be found other than his twin brother. Because the twins were seven years old their parents were asking the court to rule if Derrick's decision to give one of his kidneys to his brother, Darren, was legal. "I want Darren to have my right kidney. It's my best one," Derrick was quoted as saying. "I write with my right hand and I throw a ball with my right hand. So my right one has to be my best kidney."[1]

That is how God gives to us. He sees our need and gives his very best. God does not shy away from our need or merely offer words of encouragement from a distance. He comes himself in Christ at tremendous cost to himself, experiencing tremendous pain and loss, in order to provide the answer to our problem.

## Love Acts!

God's response to human need is the basis of the biblical mandate to involve ourselves in the needs of others. He calls us to the same costly love. Empathy is not enough. To love the way God loves, we must be willing to address the needs around us in practical ways.

In our culture a "loving person" is often viewed as mild mannered, easily swayed, someone who is more "doormat" than warrior. Kindness is often viewed as weakness. The truth is that love is the most powerful force in the world. The writer of Song of Songs understood that "love is as strong as death.... Many waters cannot quench love; rivers cannot sweep it away" (8:6–7). Love is shaped by a sense of righteousness and justice, and it cannot sit idly by while human need remains unanswered. Love isn't mild; it has a powerful impact as Jesus himself demonstrates.

I recently received a Jesus action figure as a gift. I wasn't sure what to make of it. It was strange gift. I studied the figure and the packaging carefully. It occurred to me how thoroughly the historical Jesus exceeds any imaginary action hero in power, brilliance, and by his mastery and control over creation. It brought to mind a couple of articles I read recently suggesting that what men really need is a rough-and-tumble, exceedingly manly version of Jesus. They argued that adolescent males need to hear about the calming of the storm and the clearing of the temple, not about his love for children and his tears at the death of a friend. I agree that his strength must be understood. But there is room for caution in such an approach. What one encounters today through pop theology, celebrity biography, and political ideology is a Jesus made all over again in our image, who just happens to champion all our pet projects. What we need today is not an action figure Jesus or a designer Jesus we believe meets the needs of the moment; we need to encounter the three-dimensional and living Jesus who emerges from the pages of the Gospels with power and tenderness, anger and love, divinity and humanity.

On Christmas Sunday morning I was saying good-bye to people at the church's main entrance and stated to a family who have attended the church for some time that I loved them. On Tuesday when I returned to my office I had an e-mail awaiting me from the husband of that family written Christmas morning.

Dear Phil,

I wanted to let you know how much it affected me when you said "I love you guys" as we left. No man (including my father) whom I look up to and respect as much as I do you has *ever* said that to me. That was the absolute first time I have ever heard that addressed to me (not counting my mother, my wife, kids or siblings). I also have never felt the way that made me feel. It is just different coming from someone I look up to and respect. I just wanted to thank you.

The reason I share this is that what touched my friend so deeply was not just love and not just strength, but love experienced in the context of perceived strength. I had experienced a lot of male strength as a child and often had been hurt by it. I had experienced love and at times didn't know what to do with it. It was love in the context of strength that proved transforming and inspired trust. This is the kind of love people have always received from Jesus—a strong love.

The apostle John wrote, "This is how we know what love is: Jesus Christ laid down his life for us." We know what real love looks like because of the actions of Jesus Christ in dying on the cross. But it is not enough to know about his love. John went on to say, "And we ought to lay down our lives for one another." It's not enough to be able to understand and explain the message of God's love. We must also live out God's love. If we see our sister or our brother in need and do nothing about it, we cannot argue that God's love is at work in our lives. Real love is not expressed just with words, but with actions consistent with the truth (1 John 3:16–18). As Proverbs states: "Do not withhold good from those to whom it is due, when it is in your power to act. Do not say to your neighbor, 'Come back tomorrow and I'll give it to you'—when you already have it with you" (Prov. 3:27–28). Jesus invites us to follow him in learning to love in some unlikely places.

Jesus championed unpopular causes and loved people considered beyond the reach of God's love.

One of the most appalling ideas I've heard expressed by religious people in recent years is the suggestion that AIDS is somehow God's punishment for homosexuality. I'm embarrassed to acknowledge that anyone would say this. The idea lacks a sense of reality for many reasons. It lacks compassion. It fails to see that AIDS is a terrible, insidious disease that leads to incredible human suffering. It ignores the fact that in other parts of the world AIDS is predominantly a heterosexual disease, threatening the whole of sub-Sahara Africa. (Around 180,000 children are orphaned every month by AIDS in Africa.) Such a thought fails to take into account one's own moral failure and may be an endeavor to convince ourselves that the sins of others are worse than our own. It puts in human mouths the kind of judging that only God can do.

I remember the first time I cared for a patient with AIDS. I was a first-year medical student on a clinical medicine rotation at Los Angeles County Hospital. Anthony was seventeen, very ill and depressed, experiencing all of the worst effects of advanced disease. He didn't have a lot to say at first. As I took the obligatory history I was troubled by the story that unfolded. Rejected by his family because of his sexual orientation, he had lived on the street for years, often working as a prostitute. He had been diagnosed just two years earlier. Now he spent more and more time in the hospital. Fewer and fewer people came to see him. He expressed no anger or disappointment, only loneliness and hopelessness.

I struggled inside to find ways to convey to him God's care and my own desire to offer some reason for hope. I realized how much more Jesus cared about his precious life than I had. I felt a kind of distance during the first few minutes of the encounter. It is difficult to love when we don't understand what is needed, in situations we have not encountered before. Any detachment quickly melted away, however, as I felt Anthony's pain and loss and realized his needs were just like mine. It seems to me that AIDS may be one of the greatest opportunities God's people have ever had to act with practical love, to care for people who are loved by God beyond our comprehension. Even a cursory reading of the Gospels shows us that if Jesus were walking in our shoes today, he would be in the front lines of those ministering to people struggling with this horrible disease. Love acts.

## Love Fulfills the Law

A crucial manifestation of love is that it always acts in the best interest of the beloved. This truth is expressed in the relationship between love and the law. Every law is given for one of three reasons: either it is given to protect our relationship with God, to protect our relationships with other people, or to keep us safe spiritually. God gives us the law as a guardrail to keep us from plunging over the edge into disaster. It functions positively and graciously in preventing sin-damaged people from doing further damage to themselves and their relationships. When love is functioning well in a human life, when you love other people as God loves them, love fulfills all of the law, because both the law and love are expressions of God's righteousness, justice, and mercy:

> You, my brothers and sisters, were called to be free. But do not use your freedom to indulge the sinful nature; rather, serve one another humbly in love. For the entire law is fulfilled in keeping this one command: "Love your neighbor as yourself." (Gal. 5:13–14)

> Let no debt remain outstanding, except the continuing debt to love one another, for whoever loves others has fulfilled the law. The commandments, "You shall not commit adultery," "You shall not murder," "You shall not steal," "You shall not covet," and whatever other command there may be, are summed up in this one command: "Love your neighbor as yourself." Love does no harm to its neighbor. Therefore love is the fulfillment of the law. (Rom. 13:8–10)

> One of them, an expert in the law, tested him with this question: "Teacher, which is the greatest commandment in the Law?" Jesus replied: "'Love the Lord your God with all your heart and with all your soul and with all your mind.' This is the first and greatest commandment. And the second is like it: 'Love your neighbor as yourself.' All the Law and the Prophets hang on these two commandments." (Matt. 22:35–40)

The law is an expression of the righteousness and justice of God *and* it is perfectly fulfilled in loving others. It is not possible to passively express the righteousness and justice of God. There is more to fulfilling the law than avoiding hurtful behavior. Love not only avoids harming its neighbor, it discharges every debt. Loving others involves the choice to "serve one another in love" and to love others the way we want to be loved ourselves. Christian freedom involves moving beyond the need to live in a cordoned-off area defined by the law into the joy of moving through the whole world guided by a heart transformed by the love of God. God's love erases the imaginary line between the sacred and the secular.

In Jesus' parable in Matthew 25, the eternal destiny of the "sheep" and the "goats" is determined solely on what people did or did not do for "the least of these." What did you do with the hungry and the thirsty, the stranger, the naked, the sick, and the prisoner (Matt. 25:31–46)? Jesus was not arguing for salvation by good works; he wanted us to understand that our actions reveal what is in our hearts. "Good people bring good things out of the good stored up in their heart, and evil people bring evil things out of the evil stored up in their heart. For out of the overflow of the heart the mouth speaks" (Luke 6:45).

## The Importance of Kindness

When we think about the way our lives have been impacted by the love of other people, what we usually remember is some expression of kindness we have been shown—in the form of words, attitudes, or actions. Kindness is the way we make love real to other people.

In the 1954 classic *Marty*, Ernest Borgnine plays the leading role for which he won the Academy Award for Best Actor. Marty Pelleti is a thirty-four-year-old butcher living with his mother in the Bronx. He is painfully shy, sees himself as unattractive, and has experienced enough rejection that he has lost all hope of finding the right person, while experiencing great pressure from his family to get married. One Saturday night at the "Stardust Ballroom," he witnesses a young woman being dumped for a woman her date considers more attractive. Marty seeks to comfort her and invites Clara to dance. While dancing he attempts to offer some encouragement:

> I'm having a very good time with you right now.... You see, you're not such a dog as you think you are.... I guess I'm not such a dog as I think I am.... My father was a real ugly man but my mother adored him. She told me how she used to get so miserable sometimes—like everybody, you know? And, she says my father always tried to understand. I used to see them sometimes when I was a kid sitting in the living room talking and talking. And I used to adore my old man because he was always so kind. That's one of the most beautiful things I have in my life—the way my father and mother were. And my father was a real ugly man.[2]

He says that he adored his father because of his kindness, that the most beautiful memories of his life were made possible because of his father's kindness. Are we leaving our families and friends the legacy and beauty of a life characterized by kindness?

## Expressions of Kindness

Through the years I have noticed that some people never lack for friends. They seem to know instinctively how to treat others well and foster friendship. It is a mistake to argue that this capacity for friendship is merely the result of understanding certain principles that can be learned and practiced by anyone. These things must flow from a genuinely loving heart. We are wired in such a way that we instinctively know when we are being truly loved and when we are not. There are specific ways of expressing what is in our hearts that can help us connect deeply with other people, allowing them to know that they are loved and valued. Alan Loy McGinnis's excellent book *The Friendship Factor* provides a broader and more detailed discussion of these essential skills. These actions come down to simple kindness and practical caring.

*Being generous.* One tangible expression of kindness is generosity. Paul wrote to the Corinthian church about the importance of generosity. The church in Jerusalem faced famine, and Paul was challenging other churches to respond to their need. He pointed the Corinthians to the example of the Macedonian church. "In the midst of a very severe trial, their overflowing joy and their extreme poverty welled up in rich generosity. For I testify that they gave as much as they were able, and even beyond their ability. Entirely on their own, they urgently pleaded with us for the privilege of sharing in this service" (2 Cor. 8:2–4). Out of their poverty they gave beyond what they were able to give by any human standard. Then Paul reminded the Corinthians of the example of Jesus. "For you know the grace of our Lord Jesus Christ, that though he was rich, yet for your sake he became poor, so that you through his poverty might become rich" (2 Cor. 8:9). You are to be generous, Paul argued, because God in Christ has been so generous with you.

Later in chapter 9 Paul picked up the argument again. "Remember this: Whoever sows sparingly will also reap sparingly, and whoever sows generously will also reap generously" (2 Cor. 9:6). The promise of a good return is not offered as a motivation for giving but as a statement of fact about the nature of generosity. People with a generous spirit experience generosity in their relationships. The only adequate motive for generosity is a grateful, cheerful heart (2 Cor. 9:7).

When my older brother and I were about twelve and eleven we decided together that for Christmas we each wanted a small reel-to-reel tape recorder we found on the cover of the Radio Shack catalog, just fourteen dollars and fifty cents. My father had a union job; the unions were on strike that fall and my father had no work. My mother let us know that it was not likely that they would be able to afford such gifts for us. On Christmas morning we woke up anticipating disappointment, only to find the recorders under the tree. Later my mother shared with me that two days before Christmas a missionary couple home from the field had heard about our situation and had come to our home and given money to my mother to buy presents for her five children. To this day I am so moved by the memory of their generosity. They had less money than most people I knew, but out of their poverty they gave more than they could afford to give and made me very rich.

*Making relationship a priority.* Relationships take time. The replacement of quantity of time with "quality time" is a modern myth. Many things clamor for our attention at any given moment, but few are as essential to our happiness as significant relationships. We all need close friends—people we can count on, people who know our story and who are willing to share their stories with us. These relationships require time—to open our hearts, explore the world together in conversation, wonder over the mysteries of life, and do the difficult but joyous work of loving and caring.

Hurry kills love. Hurry fills us up with the importance of our own agenda and squeezes love out of the picture.

I was sitting in our most comfortable chair reading the paper after a long and tiring day, feeling that my emotional resources were completely depleted. Jonathan, who was three at the time, came into the room and began to say something to me about one of his toys, and I responded with impatience. "Just wait a minute, wait a minute. Let me finish reading this." This is one of the early indicators of a hurried life—living a pace of life that leaves only emotional leftovers for those at home who need us most. I had snapped at Jonathan several times when it occurred to me what I was doing. I was conveying to my son that the newspaper was more important to me than he was. Sometimes kindness comes down to little, practical things like setting down the newspaper and giving our undivided attention to the people we love.

*Listening.* People need to be heard. Everyone has a story to tell but there are so few people willing to listen. Even in good friendships we can be so full of our own thoughts that we are constantly preparing our next sentence rather taking in the other person's words. Jesus demonstrates a tremendous capacity for listening. He often asked questions and allowed people to tell their story.

Listening is enhanced by a number of simple skills. Ask questions and demonstrate a genuine interest in the other person. Make eye contact. Leave plenty of room for others to finish their thoughts. Don't interrupt. Don't be too quick to respond with advice or opinions. What people need most is not advice but to be heard. Prove yourself a trustworthy person by keeping to yourself whatever someone shares with you in confidence. Good listening is an expression of genuine humility. It allows others to know they have worth and value because someone was willing to set aside the importance of their own thoughts, opinions, feelings and reputation long enough to embrace the words and story of someone else.

*Openness and vulnerability.* Taking on the weight of another's burdens fulfills Jesus' command that we love each other in the way we have been loved by him. Burden-bearing implies burden-sharing. We can't care for each other without sharing our needs.

I am drawn to those who are open and vulnerable with me. In my experience, when people honestly share their brokenness with me, my respect for them grows. Such honesty in another person provides the sense that it is safe to be honest with them in return. As a physician I have found that openness with my patients helps provide a place of openness for them. As a pastor I recognize the importance of my openness and vulnerability with our church family in encouraging their openness with one another, inviting them to see my need for God's work in my own heart, and in my passionate concern to avoid the obvious pitfalls of pride and hypocrisy.

Recently I spoke to a group of nurses about end-of-life issues and the importance of advanced directives. In the process I shared two experiences of losing people I love. One nurse opened up about the recent loss of her husband. Before I was out the door five different people stopped me and shared quite openly their own loss of a loved one and thanked me for the way my openness had helped them.

Jesus invited broken people into friendship by his openness. His anger, tears, and joy were never hidden. He continually opened his heart to the Twelve—struggling, laughing, praying, crying, pleading. "I no longer call you servants, because servants do not know their master's business. Instead, I have called you friends, for everything that I learned from my Father I have made known to you" (John 15:15).

*Affirmation and encouragement.* We celebrate victories together when we are on the same team, but all too often we find ourselves in a culture of competition and comparison where it is difficult to celebrate the successes of others. This is tragic because words of encouragement have a powerful effect upon the human soul.

I owe a great deal of my spiritual well-being to the church where I met Jesus Christ and grew up spiritually. I arrived there a very broken youth and immediately found some people who genuinely cared about me.

One of those people was my fifth-grade Sunday school teacher, Brice Carlson. He went out of his way to care for the guys in that class. On Sunday mornings, Brice and his wife, Carolyn, would often have us into their home for breakfast. This was always special for me because their home was a warm and peaceful place. They had two daughters who were a few years older than I was. Brice always spoke to them with such kindness and respect, often referring to them as "Sweetie." He was a burly, hardworking contractor, but thoroughly kind and tender. People know when they are being truly loved and when they are not, and with Brice I was always fairly certain that he loved me. I remember the day as a teenager when, in a conversation, he spontaneously addressed me as "Sweetie." I had never heard him use that term with anyone but his daughters. As a teenager I had no desire to be called "Sweetie." But that single word brought more healing to my heart than I can now describe. To this day he calls me "Sweetie," and I can hardly speak of it without tears.

*Affection and appropriate touch.* Mr. Osipov was in many ways the toughest patient I ever admitted to the hospital. A Russian-Armenian, he refused to speak a word of English. At sixty-seven he had a strong, muscular, square build, and multiple tattoos added to the impression of his toughness. He refused to smile and any words were gruffly barked. The message was clear: No one was getting inside.

He came to the hospital late at night because of severe abdominal pain. I knew he would be with us for a few days and I was determined to win him over. Throughout the initial exam he refused all efforts at kindness. When I said "good night" I placed my hands around both ankles and gave him a firm affectionate squeeze. No response. On rounds the next morning I was met with the same attitude and demeanor. On the way out of the room I reached down and squeezed his big toe through the covers. From that time on I did the same thing every time I left his room. About the fifth time he anticipated my move and moved his foot quickly to avoid my squeeze. But I found his toe. The next visit ended the same way. He struggled even more to avoid my grasp, but as I reached his toe he began to laugh. It was all over. From that point on I have been his friend and physician. His heart has softened over time at many levels.

Appropriate touch conveys affection and helps us feel connected.

## Kindness and Children

Often, parents get impatient with their children not because the children are doing something wrong but simply because their behavior is inconvenient. Especially with very young children it's easy for our communication to become largely negative, with a steady stream of "no" and other denials. Yet children desperately need affirmation and encouragement. We may need to stem the tide of negative feedback by offering constructive alternatives, allowing ourselves to be inconvenienced by just getting down on the floor and playing with our children, or by being willing to pick them up more often. I'm not talking about making our children the center of the universe, giving in to every whim or spoiling the child. I simply want to encourage kindness, respect, and clearer understanding of the needs of the child. Sometimes parenting can place us in a battle of conflicting needs. Who is going to be the servant?

I agree with C. S. Lewis that the most concerning behavior I witness in families is usually not children toward parents but parents toward their children. Parents may speak to their children with tremendous incivility and disrespect because they assume that their role as adults allows them to do so. There is a reason many children don't want to be home and would rather be anywhere else.[3] Our manners at home with the people we know best are pretty good indicators of our real character.

Children need to hear their parents speak to each other with kindness and respect. This is crucial to establishing an atmosphere of security where children can develop trust and confidence. Harsh and disrespectful words are a burden that children should not have to carry.

And don't discipline in the heat of anger. When we discipline in anger it is easy to voice our frustration and to attend to some need in ourselves, addressing and venting our own pain and frustration, while failing to address the child's need for nurture and direction. We need to take a moment to calm down and catch our breath, to be sure that we are disciplining out of love and seeking the best interest of our children. They will know the difference.

## Sacrifice

The call of Jesus is an invitation to spend and be spent, to give our lives away in meeting the needs of the world.

I think one of the greatest analogies of God's love is the response of parents and spouses in caring for a severely ill child or spouse. To watch a relationship where so much is required that was not anticipated; where the cost can be so great; where there is so much pain, worry, time, and energy that must be expended; but where love and care are given gladly because of love itself, not merely out of a sense of responsibility or obligation, is a sacred experience. When we see such commitment and care between people, I think we are seeing God's love in human lives at its best. People who go through such experiences are champions of love and some of the great heroes of humanity.

God asks us to love a hurting and broken world like that. It is a world of billions of lonely, struggling people like us looking for a reason for hope. Perhaps it will be some expression of God's kindness through us that provides the basis for their hope in the only one who can make us whole.

People are hungry for kindness. A kind person harnesses the power of God in both actions and words. This person is a compelling agent of transformation. People cannot hear the Christian message until they see it in a human life. They will not recognize us as followers of Jesus until we love the way he does. Kindness causes hearts to open and words take on increased value. Our actions begin to tell the story of God's kindness, and if our words are also motivated by love our message takes on tremendous integrity.

It's not enough to tell people that God loves them. They need to see that love acting through us. They need to know that we love them.

# —Making Love Real—

The fruit of the Spirit called kindness is important because it is the way we make God's love real to each other.

Ask God to lead you to someone this week who needs to be loved in a real, practical way. Ask God to show you a way to demonstrate his kindness to that person.

# 10

# No Safe Investments: Trust

The late morning and afternoon were spent playing in the neighbor's pool. Our mothers sat at the end of the pool talking and keeping watch. Eventually, it was time to go home. I was three and can't remember what I was thinking, but after everyone else was out the gate, I jumped into the deep end. I remember that experience vividly—swallowing water, sinking, wave after wave of panic. The neighbor's son heard something fall into the water and went back to take a look. Thankfully, he pulled me to safety. Soon after that I learned to swim, but I had already determined never again to venture out into water that was deeper than I could stand up in.

Life can be shaped by such experiences. The experience of the present moment is filtered through the pain, loss, and disappointments of the past. These past experiences can lead to patterns of self-protection. I know that the pain and disappointments in my own life have driven me at times to keep my distance, to avoid pain by failing to invest. The pain in our lives can lead us away from the sacrifice and commitment essential to love. We are afraid to move into the deeper waters, to risk the pain that comes with love, choosing the safety of the familiar and predictable.

What are we to do with our pain and disappointment? How can we find the courage to move toward a deepening capacity for love?

## The Necessity of Trust

As we struggle with the pain of a failed adoption, I find myself contemplating the way Jesus struggled with his Father's will in the garden of Gethsemane. I am helped by what I see there. What I am experiencing right now is not a crisis of faith but an experience of deep pain that causes me to struggle with God's will. It's hard for all of us to understand at times why things have to be the way they are. I remember how Jesus said, "My soul is overwhelmed with sorrow to the point of death. Stay here and keep watch with me" (Matt. 26:38). I can't fully understand what his soul must have felt, but I do know what it is to feel overwhelmed with sadness, and it helps me to know that the one who is in charge of my life is no stranger to these feelings.

Facing the suffering and shame of a sin-bearing death, Jesus asked that "the cup" be taken away "if possible." In other words, *If there's a plan B this would be a great time to know about it. But my intentions are to do what you will, Father, no matter what.* Later, he prayed, "My Father, if it is not possible for this cup to be taken away unless I drink it, may your will be done" (Matt. 26:42). In that statement, Jesus took another step toward acceptance. There was never a question of whether or not he would obey. Each time the bottom line was the same. *What you want, Father, that is what I'm going to do.*

It helps me to see that this wasn't just stoic resignation. There was a real struggle involved in facing the pain and anguish that would come with obedience. We see a progressive acceptance on his part leading to action. In the end he responds to his Father's will by walking right into the hands of those who wanted to kill him. "No one takes [my life] from me," Jesus said, "but I lay it down of my own accord" (John 10:18). Jesus embraced his Father's will with the suffering and the pain of the cross.

Hebrews 5 contains the briefest account of the Garden of Gethsemane in the New Testament. The writer of Hebrews described Jesus' experience: "During the days of Jesus' life on earth, he offered up prayers and petitions with fervent cries and tears to the one who could save him from death, and he was heard because of his reverent submission. Son though he was, he learned obedience from what he suffered" (vv. 7–8). Why did Jesus choose the path of love? Why was he able to choose the path of sacrifice when he dreaded it so much? The writer of Hebrews explained Jesus' choice: He was confident that his Father could deliver him from death. He trusted his Father, and so he obeyed.

Peter expressed this same thought more explicitly: "To this you were called, because Christ suffered for you, leaving you an example, that you should follow in his steps. 'He committed no sin, and no deceit was found in his mouth.' When they hurled their insults at him, he did not retaliate; when he suffered, he made no threats." Why didn't he retaliate? Why didn't he fight back? Peter explained, "Instead, he entrusted himself to him who judges justly" (1 Peter 2:21–23). Instead of abandoning the course of obedience and self-sacrifice, Jesus made the choice to trust his Father.

I reached around the corner into my closet to grab a necktie in a hurry to get to church early one Sunday morning. Jonathan, who was two and clad only in his diaper, moved silently across the room. I didn't hear him coming. As I turned, my knee caught his right cheek, lifting him off the ground and hurling him onto the floor a few feet away. I picked him up, my own heart pierced by the pain he must have felt, the pain I had caused. Not knowing what else to say I asked, "Are you okay?" His only response was simply, "Yup."

A lump was already forming on his chin. Jonathan, who was expert at crying out heartily whenever the occasion warranted, lay quietly in my arms. His eyes were tearing but the look on his face was one of contentment. He never cried. As I looked into those big brown eyes and past them into his precious heart, I thought for a moment that I understood. It was as if he were saying, "My father did this to me. My father has never hurt me. My father would never hurt me. I must not be hurt." His trust is one of the most precious and generous gifts I had ever received.

Jesus' unyielding commitment to doing his Father's will grew out of the way he trusted his Father. This is crucial to living a life of love. If we're not trusting God's goodness and his ability to take care of us, we will always gravitate toward taking care of ourselves.

## Learning to Trust

In one of the most candid letters of all time to a supporting church, Paul described his situation like this: "We were under great pressure, far beyond our ability to endure, so that we despaired of life itself. Indeed, we felt we had received the sentence of death" (2 Cor. 1:8–9). Now that seems like just the right thing to say if you want to get called home from the field. But Paul's honesty about his own struggle brought new hope to the struggling church because it was expressed against the backdrop of God's character. "But this happened that we might not rely on ourselves but on God, who raises the dead. He has delivered us from such a deadly peril, and he will deliver us again" (2 Cor. 1:9–10). Paul responded to the Father in the same way Jesus did—with heroic obedience flowing from trust and confidence in God.

In Psalm 25, David wrote, "My eyes are ever on the LORD, for only he will release my feet from the snare" (v. 15). David described the posture of trust. Life is full of potential problems and "snares." We can live focused downward on our feet, carefully choosing each step in an effort to manage our own safety and security. But when you're looking down all the time you lose a sense of orientation and run into things. There is another choice. Keep your eyes on the Lord, follow his lead, and trust that he will take care of your steps and lead you where you are supposed to go.

It is easy to let our problems define us. We focus on them, plan, worry, fret, obsess. We can hold our problems so close to our eyes that they are all we see. We can come to believe at times that there is not a whole lot more to our lives than our problems. But if we were to hold them up high against the backdrop of God's character, the vastness of his being, his power, competence, mercy, and gracious intentions, all of a sudden we regain perspective. Our problems take on proper proportion and we are freed to move forward.

Paul described followers of Jesus as rejoicing even in the middle of serious problems and struggle (Rom.

5:1–5). He did not encourage us to live in denial, but rather to hold our struggles in an eternal perspective:

- For the *past* we have forgiveness and reconciliation: "We have peace with God" (Rom. 5:1).
- In the *present* moment we have "access by faith into this grace in which we now stand" (Rom. 5:2). We have a relationship with a Father to whom we can come confidently and joyfully at any time.
- And for the *future* we anticipate "the hope of the glory of God" (Rom. 5:2).

Paul's argument, simply stated, is this: The biggest problem we ever had, a problem exponentially bigger than any other problem we will ever have—our sin, spiritual death, and separation from God—has been answered by God himself. Because of Jesus, God is our Father. Our sins are forgiven. Death no longer gets the final word. This is the most important and best conceivable news we will ever hear, and because this is true we can live with genuine joy even in the middle of real problems.

The invitation of faith is not to denial. It is a call to see our problems in their proper context.

## The Origins of Trust

Erik Erikson, describing the earliest stages of human development, emphasized the importance of "basic trust," an essential component of maturity and emotional health. When parents prove trustworthy through sensitive care and consistency, the child cultivates a capacity for trust and for expressing a potential for significant interactions with others. David wrote that we learn to trust at our mother's breast (Ps. 22:9). This process begins in the earliest moments of life, and if this stage in life is not successfully negotiated it can lead to basic mistrust, expressed as a tendency to turn inward and an impaired ability to trust and to form attachments with other people.[1]

In the last few decades, through understanding the effects of institutionalization on orphaned infants from Romania and parts of the former Soviet Union, we have a clearer understanding of the importance of love in human development. Many of these children develop problems centered around emotional disturbances, developmental delays, and learning disabilities. Some adapt and seem to do fine. But the effects of multiple caregivers, shortage of personnel, absence of appropriate touch, and insufficient response to need is clearly devastating for many.

As infants we are helpless. We have no control over our environment and depend on someone to provide care, feed, hold, warm, and protect us. Our only responses to the world are reflexive expressions of need. We can cry, suck, grasp. And when we do these things we need a response. If we cry, someone feeds us. If we grab a finger, it stays there until we let it go. If we smile or make a cute sound, someone smiles and makes sounds back. And so we learn that we have an effect on our environment and we begin to make sense out of the pattern of care and response we receive. With time we begin to form attachments to those who care for us consistently. Those who care for us help shape our view of the world. Responsiveness and consistency provide a basis for trust and security. Once we feel a little secure we begin to venture out, often seeking a visual connection with the ones we trust, a familiar face and expressions of assurance.

What if when we cried no one responded and our most basic needs were met only when it was convenient for someone else? Infants who experience such lack of care begin to shut down, appearing unemotional, and fail to learn to interact with others and to regulate their responses.[2]

John addressed this roadblock to a growing capacity for relationship and love when he referred to those who "fear" as people "not made perfect in love" (1 John 4:18). He argued that even if we struggle with an impaired ability to trust we have another opportunity to negotiate this part of our development by encountering God's love for us.

God is gentle, loving, and meticulous in his care. He promises his people, "As a mother comforts her child, so I will comfort you" (Isa. 66:13). He is a parent who will never let us down. He will always answer when we call. He can be trusted.

# Love Is Risky

C. S. Lewis, reflecting on St. Augustine's experience at the death of his friend Nebridius, described himself as easily moved to tears by this section of *The Confessions*. Augustine openly expressed profound grief in words that are frank and deeply moving.

> Everything I had shared with my friend turned into hideous anguish without him. My eyes sought him everywhere, but he was missing ... Weeping alone brought me solace, and took my friend's place as the only comfort of my soul ... I was miserable, and miserable too is everyone whose mind is chained by friendship with mortal things, and is torn apart by their loss ...
>
> Woe to the madness which thinks to cherish human beings as though more than human! How foolish the human heart that anguishes without restraint over human ills, as I did then! Feverishly I thrashed about, sighed, wept and was troubled, and there was no repose for me, nor any counsel. Within me I was carrying a tattered, bleeding soul that did not want me to carry it, yet I could find no place to lay it down.[3]

Augustine concluded that we must never give our hearts to anything but the eternal God who will never pass away. Lewis said that although this makes excellent sense to our human nature, it leaves us "a thousand miles away from Christ."[4]

I must confess to a tendency toward being a safety-first creature. My cautious side has been intensified at times by the traumatic aspects of life I have witnessed in the emergency room. I want the people I care about to be safe. I want to be safe. We instinctively avoid unnecessary loss; this is what motivated Augustine's conclusion.

In the end Lewis viewed Augustine's conclusion as a "hangover from the high-minded Pagan philosophies in which he grew up." Lewis went on to say,

> There is no escape along the lines St. Augustine suggests. Nor along any other lines. There is no safe investment. To love at all is to be vulnerable. Love anything, and your heart will certainly be wrung and possibly be broken. If you want to make sure of keeping it intact, you must give your heart to no one, not even to an animal. Wrap it carefully round with hobbies and little luxuries; avoid all entanglements; lock it up safe in the casket or coffin of your selfishness. But in that casket—safe, dark, motionless, airless—it will change. It will not be broken; it will become unbreakable, impenetrable, irredeemable. The alternative to tragedy, or at least to the risk of tragedy, is damnation. The only place outside Heaven where you can be perfectly safe from all the dangers and perturbations of love is Hell.[5]

To love is to suffer in a fallen world. There are no safe investments. There are no safe relationships. In this world there are no investments of love that come with a guarantee that you will not be hurt and disappointed. But Jesus' command to us is to love one another, to risk love.

Other than Carole, no one on the planet has greater power to bring me joy and blessing than my children. This is true because I love them so much. But because I love them it is also true that there is no one who has more potential for bringing me pain and suffering. Both things are true. They come together. They are opposite sides of the same coin. But I would never choose against having them as my children because of the pain they might bring. I choose love in spite of the risk. Love involves a trade-off between joy and the possibility of suffering and loss. Evelyn Underhill wrote, "Pain, or at least the willingness to risk pain, alone gives dignity to human love, and it is the price of its creative power. Without this, it is mere emotional enjoyment. It costs much to love any human being to the bitter end; and on every plane a total generosity, a love that includes pain and embraces it, is the price of all genuine accomplishment."[6]

Love trusts God with the outcome. Without trusting God, we run the risk of always being "calculating." In fact, the only alternative to trusting God with the outcome is to live as a calculating person. We will tend to view people as a means to an end rather than an end in themselves.[7] To God people are the end, and we are to love them as he has loved them.

One popular message in the church today is the emphasis on "boundaries." Though having healthy boundaries is certainly important, my concern with this movement is that its message will be co-opted by the natural bent of the sin-damaged human spirit, leading us away from investing in others and toward greater and greater levels of self-protection. If we learn to tidy up our boundaries without simultaneously

learning to be loving servants we may merely be legit-
imizing our selfishness.

The message of the kingdom of God is not of building better walls, but of building bigger hearts, more
inclusive hearts, and tearing down the walls that
divide. Where in the life of the church are we encouraging the sacrificial living to which Jesus calls?

The most worthwhile things in life are risky, and
that is proven to us by the vulnerability of God who
comes in Jesus Christ and waits for our response. Have
you ever pondered how vulnerable God has made himself? He laid it all out there. He paid everything to
restore our relationship to him, and now he says, "How
will you respond? What will you do with the love that
has cost me so much?" What incredible vulnerability.

When we look at the vulnerability of Jesus, the way
he loved and served and gave himself away, it is tempting to feel, *Wow! If I loved like that, the way Jesus loves,
I could lose everything. I could lose my life.* And you
would be right. The irony is that this is the life he
invites us to live. Jesus said, "Whoever wants to be my
disciple must deny themselves and take up their cross
daily and follow me. For whoever wants to save their
life will lose it, but whoever loses their life for me will
save it" (Luke 9:23–24).

What really matters is not our accomplishments
but our relationships. To be committed to this principle is to sacrifice a large degree of control. We can
manage our accomplishments to a certain degree, but
we cannot manage relationships in the same way. Trust

is essential, trust that our Father will take care of us, the kind of trust that would allow us to live like Jesus. Paul wrote, "Walk in the way of love, just as Christ loved us and gave himself up for us as a fragrant offering and sacrifice to God" (Eph. 5:2).

Every day we all face a simple choice between remaining safe and the risk of generously loving. Will we follow Jesus into a life of love? Will we make the choice to lose our lives? Will we allow him to live his life in us? Will we allow ourselves to spend and be spent for the sake of the world? The answer will depend upon our choice to trust him.

I had spent the morning in the shallow end of the pool. At nine, I could swim like a fish and loved the water. But I feared the deep end. It was a beautiful late-summer day. Arnie Richter had invited all of the guys in the fifth and sixth grades at church to use his hillside pool. Arnie was a strapping bear of a man in his thirties, always caring and encouraging. He was there to supervise and had noticed my self-imposed limitations. In the middle of the day he called me over and asked me to do something. "You go to the deep end of the pool. I'll stand here and you swim across the pool to me." I explained my hesitation, but he insisted. "I'll be right here for you. I won't let anything happen." I stood at the opposite end of the pool for quite some time, embarrassed by my fear and resistance. Minutes passed. Arnie waited patiently. I loved Arnie and I trusted him. I knew he would be there for me. Suddenly an impulse emerged from somewhere deep inside and I took the leap of faith. I hit the water, heart pounding, arms and legs urgently flailing; seconds later my arm hit the other end of the pool. I would never fear the deeper water again.

God is calling us forward. He asks us to risk love. He is calling us into the deeper water. He offers us his presence and the promise that he will never abandon us. It's time to trust. It's time to jump in.

# —Making Love Real—

Trusting God is essential to a growing capacity for loving. Read Psalm 27 several times today. It is a wonderful expression of confidence in God's watchful care. Make it a prayer as you read. Ask God to fill your heart with a sense of trust and confidence in him. If there are issues that make trust difficult for you, talk with God about those things and ask him to demonstrate his faithfulness to you in those places in your heart.

# Part Three

# How Does Love Grow?

Shout it aloud, do not hold back. Raise your voice like a trumpet. Declare to my people their rebellion and to the house of Jacob their sins. For day after day they seek me out; they seem eager to know my ways, as if they were a nation that does what is right and has not forsaken the commands of its God.

They ask me for just decisions and seem eager for God to come near them. "Why have we fasted," they say, "and you have not seen it? Why have we humbled ourselves, and you have not noticed?"

Yet on the day of your fasting, you do as you please and exploit all your workers. Your fasting ends in quarreling and strife, and in striking each other with wicked fists. You cannot fast as you do today and expect your voice to be heard on high. Is this the kind of fast I have chosen, only a day for people to humble themselves? Is it only for bowing one's head like a reed and for lying in sackcloth and ashes? Is that what you call a fast, a day acceptable to the LORD?

Is not this the kind of fasting I have chosen: to loose the chains of injustice and untie the cords of the yoke, to set the oppressed free and break every yoke?

Is it not to share your food with the hungry and to provide the poor wanderer with shelter — when you see the naked, to clothe them, and not to turn away from your own flesh and blood?

Then your light will break forth like the dawn, and your healing will quickly appear; then your righteousness will go before you, and the glory of the LORD will be your rear guard. Then you will call, and the LORD will answer; you will cry for help, and he will say: Here am I.

If you do away with the yoke of oppression, with the pointing finger and malicious talk, and if you spend yourselves in behalf of the hungry and satisfy the needs of the oppressed, then your light will rise in the darkness, and your night will become like the noonday.

The LORD will guide you always; he will satisfy your needs in a sun-scorched land and will strengthen your frame. You will be like a well-watered garden, like a spring whose waters never fail.

Your people will rebuild the ancient ruins and will raise up the age-old foundations; you will be called Repairer of Broken Walls, Restorer of Streets with Dwellings.

ISAIAH 58:1–12

# 11

# The Flow of Grace:
# Generosity

Eight or nine of us stood around talking after evening worship in front of the church where I grew up spiritually. Gene, a good friend who was making a transition from the college group to a graduate age group, suggested to the others that I should take a leadership role in the college ministry. I took it as a compliment but was stunned by his reasoning. "You know, what I love about Phil is that he really loves the Lord." For me, surprisingly, the dominant feeling as I heard those words was pain. I was disappointed by my real lack of love. Feelings alone may not be the ultimate measure of love, but they are certainly not irrelevant. In that moment I did not feel anything for God that I could call love.

I know that it looked like I loved and that I acted like

I loved, but what they could not see was my heart. I was not the person Gene thought I was. I played "the impostor" and allowed the perception to stand. But it hurt. I wanted to grow in love. I wanted to experience the joy of a passionate love for God. But as I looked within, I saw the selfishness, the ulterior motives, and the capacity for manipulation.

How does love grow in a human heart? How do we become more loving? Is there a process of growth and transformation that can be defined, understood, and lived out? How will we know that our hearts are growing and changing?

# A Matter of the Heart

Love is a complex phenomenon. Earlier I suggested a working definition of godly love: Love is a commitment of the will and a joy of the spirit that expresses itself in the choice to act in the best interest of the beloved. It is a commitment of the will, a choice to serve, sacrifice, and to hang in there through thick and thin. And though commitment is foundational, love is more than commitment. In its various expressions it is often characterized by joy—the mystery and excitement of romance, the playfulness and intensity of sexuality, the goodness of friendship, the warmth of familial love. Love is a breathtaking dance between joy and commitment, play and discipline, freedom and resolve, ecstasy and agony. This is the model of all loves from the greatest Lover, who "for the *joy* set before him … *endured the cross*" (Heb. 12:2).

I was going through the motions of love, but the joy and the passion weren't there. As I examined my heart in light of the most basic understanding of love, I was exposed as a fraud. I think God must have been overjoyed by my newfound sense of need. I didn't know at the time that my quandary would set me on the path to one of life's greatest adventures.

# Choosing to Love

My experience that Sunday evening set a course leading to some major turning points in my life. What I had known deep down for a long time became painfully clear: I was a very selfish person. When I looked at my life and my world, I realized how oriented I was toward myself and my own needs. Here I was preparing for a life of service to God, wondering if there was any chance that I could be set free to live only for God's glory, to speak only to point others to him. This became a major point of discussion in prayer. For months I prayed, often on my knees for long periods of time. I was surprised by how little changed. But then one day as I was reading through my Bible, I came upon Isaiah 58 for the first time in a long time.

Speaking as God's messenger, Isaiah reflected a passionate concern over any religion that is focused on externals. He described religious behavior that imitates godliness but is unconnected to the heart as nothing but a hollow practice. Such "religious folk" look like people hungry for God, who want to know God and understand his way of doing things, but when they go home, out of the public eye, they use others for their own gain, argue, fight, and mistreat members of their own households.

In reaction to such religious display, God proclaims, "Is not this the kind of fasting I have chosen: to loose the chains of injustice and untie the cords of the yoke, to set the oppressed free and break every yoke? Is it not to share your food with the hungry and to provide the poor wanderer with shelter—when you see the naked, to clothe them, and not to turn away from your own flesh and blood?"

We are asked to choose what God chooses, to desire what God desires, to feel passionately about the things that matter to him, to give our lives to fulfilling his will. True spirituality changes our hearts and gives us a passionate concern for the things that matter to God.

As I read this chapter again, it was as if God was saying to me, *Hey! If you're really serious about wanting to become a less selfish person, I want you to start doing what a less selfish person would do.* Even in the place of prayer, I had been *saying* one thing and *willing* another.

It occurred to me that one thing a less selfish person would do is to practice generosity. Though it seemed perfunctory, I decided to start giving my things away. I found a box and began filling it with some of the things I had around my apartment. None of it seemed too special. There was a house on campus where some international students lived. I was friends with several of them and knew that they had less than I did. I felt awkward and nervous, but I could tell by Anthony's attitude that the gift was welcome. Three hours later I was still there, sharing a meal, exchanging stories, and receiving appreciation disproportionate to my actions. I feel silly even mentioning this episode except that it was pivotal. I began to pursue greater adventures. The deepest joy was to be found when no one knew what I was doing but God.

As I redirected my will and made the choice to act less selfishly and to count the needs of other people as more important than my own, God added his grace to my actions, and my heart began to change. When we choose to do his will, we free him to do a deeper work in our lives. By acting on the grace we have, we invite more grace.

In a moment of stress we may feel like speaking to someone harshly. God gives us enough grace to choose to speak with patience and kindness. If we choose to work that grace out in the moment it may seem like a small thing, but doing it two, three, ten, a hundred times over impacts who we are becoming. Oswald Chambers called this "forming habits on the basis of the grace of God."

> If we have experienced regeneration, we must not only talk about the experience ... We have to show it in our fingertips, in our tongue, and in our bodily contact with other people ... The question of forming habits on the basis of the grace of God is a very vital one. To ignore it is to fall into the snare of the Pharisee—the grace of God is praised, Jesus Christ is praised, the Redemption is praised, but the practical everyday life evades working it out. If we refuse to practice, it

is not God's grace that fails when a crisis comes, but our own nature. When the crisis comes we ask God to help us but He cannot if we have not made our nature our ally. The practicing is ours, not God's. God regenerates us and puts us in contact with all His divine resources, but He cannot make us walk according to His will.[1]

It was a baby step. I knew that. It was a simple choice to soften my heart and to allow it to be changed, and by God's grace I began to experience the world with greater sensitivity to other people. I began to change. And every day we all face the same types of choices.

# The Little Choices

Though we tend to remember our lives in terms of the big events, the reality is that life is a continuous series of seemingly insignificant choices. The sum of those choices determines who we become and the course of our lives.

Each of us has moments when we sense that we must act. We read something—perhaps we're reading Scripture or we hear a sermon or something happens in a movie—and all of a sudden the Holy Spirit places in our hearts a small vision of what could be: an *impulse to good*. We say to ourselves, "You know, I could do something about that. I could respond to that need—to seek forgiveness from a family member, to speak a word of encouragement, to visit a nursing home, to share the best and most important news I have ever heard with someone who needs to hear it." Try to remember the last time you had that experience. You see another person and recognize the need in their lives, thinking, "Whoa, I could do something about that. I could say something; I could write a note."

What do you do with that impulse to do good, which the Holy Spirit is birthing in your heart? We have several choices. We can ignore it, we can wait, or we can act on it. The choice to wait is the most common and usually leads to the same outcome as ignoring God's voice. The sin-damaged human soul is like a leaky tire. We may experience that impulse to do good, but it loses its urgency if we let it sit there long enough. It loses energy. The pressure in our souls is gone. We don't say that word; we don't write that note; we don't do what the Holy Spirit calls us to do. We don't yield. We fail to embrace the work the Holy Spirit is doing in our lives. If we want to facilitate the flow of grace, we need to listen carefully to the Holy Spirit, and we need to do what he calls us to do.

It's easier to put off doing good until that one thing changes that is going to make doing God's will easier: when I get that new job; when my spouse changes; when I have more money; when I get older. But Jesus is right here, wherever we are, through the Holy Spirit. And he is speaking now. Wherever we are, now is the time and this is the place to live in the kingdom of God.

# The Pivotal Choice

For those sincerely seeking, the prophet Isaiah has a lot to say. In Isaiah 58:9–11, he listed the concerns that must be addressed by those who are pursuing God. "If you do away with the yoke of oppression, with the pointing finger and malicious talk, and if you spend yourselves in behalf of the hungry and satisfy the needs of the oppressed, then your light will rise in the dark-ness, and your night will become like the noonday. The LORD will guide you always; he will satisfy your needs in a sun-scorched land and will strengthen your frame. You will be like a well-watered garden, like a spring whose waters never fail."

God says plainly that if you choose to pour yourself into meeting the needs of others in accordance with his will, positive consequences follow as a result of his grace. The promises are not of financial or material prosperity but of spiritual abundance. This pattern of obedience and resulting blessing repeats itself three times in the course of the chapter.

Isaiah 58 makes the point visually, graphically, plainly: We all have a choice between the parched, bone-dry, burning sands of the self-life and the vibrant, flourishing, soul-fulfilling life that God promises to those who will take up his concern for the needs of oth-ers. It is a choice between being a reservoir or a conduit. Merely taking God's blessings as ends in themselves, functioning like a receptacle or reservoir, leads to dry-ness and spiritual poverty. Becoming a channel of God's blessings, pouring those blessings out into the lives of others, leads to spiritual abundance.

If you see God's blessing as an end in itself, if you think that the point of the Christian life is for you to be forgiven, saved, and blessed, and that your main purpose in life is collecting God's blessing as in a basin, in the end you are going to end up dry and parched. But if you see yourself as a conduit or a pipe, receiving the love and grace and blessings of God and dumping that grace and mercy into the lives of others, loving the unloved, feeding the hungry, clothing the naked, caring for the oppressed, if you see that as the end and goal—to be a pipe, a conduit of God's mercy—then your life will be filled with overflowing blessing, grace, and mercy. Your life will take on the qualities of a lush garden with an endless supply of water.

Paul described his hunger to know Christ more fully by saying, "I press on to take hold of that for which Christ Jesus took hold of me" (Phil. 3:12). Jesus not only takes hold of our lives, he does it with a purpose. Our salvation and experience of God's grace is not an end in itself or the goal of our Christian experience, but the beginning of a greater work God longs to do through us. Jesus redeems us with a purpose.

Thirty years ago I brought my mother a flat of African violets that had been thrown out at the store where I worked in the afternoon during high school. They were withered and dying. Through careful attention she nursed all of them back to health, and to this day those same plants are flourishing in her living room

window. (When I was single I was given a few house-
plants through the years, and they lived exactly as long
as they can live without water.) My mother tells me that
with violets it is important not to overwater. They need
drainage holes in the bottom to let the water run out.
The human spirit is like that. We are channels,
riverbeds of the torrents of God's grace. We are not
intended to be basins. God's grace must flow through us
to others.

When I look at the lives of truly caring people I realize that they have made hundreds of choices over years
to extend themselves meaningfully into the lives of others. Do they do this because they are more loving? I
think that most of the time it works the other way. I'd
like to think that they are more loving because of their
choices to love. I describe this principle as "the flow of
grace." Understanding this principle can help us understand how one's capacity for love can grow. It opens up
key insights into the nature of transformation.

When God pours his love into our lives and we
make the choice to pour that love into someone else's
life, a new emotional and spiritual economy is established. And when all of us decide to participate in the
flow of grace, we become a community awash in grace.
Such a church is an irresistible force. I long for us to
live as people who are awash in grace because we realize that the blessings of God were never intended just
for us as an end in themselves, but that God means for
us to pass them on and pour them out into the lives of
others.

# Trusting the Adequacy of His Love

The apostle Paul understood the dynamics of the flow of grace. In 2 Corinthians 9, Paul pleaded with the church to trust in the sufficiency of the love and grace that God has poured into our lives. Paul wrote, "And God is able to bless you abundantly, so that in *all* things at *all* times, having *all* that you need, you will abound in *every* good work" (2 Cor. 9:8). The Holy Spirit will never give you an impulse to do good and not give you the grace to act on it. If you will become a conduit of God's grace in whatever God calls you to do as a servant to human need, his grace will *always* prove sufficient.

Elsewhere Paul expressed the same principle to the Thessalonians as a prayer. "With this in mind, we constantly pray for you, that our God may make you worthy of his calling, and that by his power he may bring to fruition your every desire for goodness and your every deed prompted by your faith" (2 Thess. 1:11). Paul knew that every time the Holy Spirit plants an impulse to do good in your heart, God will give you the power to live it out.

Reading between the lines of the account of the feeding of the five thousand in Matthew 14, it's fascinating to see the way in which Jesus drew his apprentices along the path of love. The disciples came to Jesus and told him what they were feeling, that all these people hanging around day and night were bothering them; they needed to eat, they wanted food, and there simply was none to be had. So they asked Jesus to "send the crowds away" (Matt. 14:15).

Have you ever felt that way? You watch the news and human need stacks up in minutes to the point of being overwhelming, and you want the whole mess just to go away. The needs are so big you feel helpless to do anything. That's how the disciples felt after a few days of intensive ministry.

But Jesus said, "They do not need to go away. You give them something to eat" (Matt. 14:16). The disciples came to Jesus with five loaves and two fish, and Jesus instructed them to seat the people in groups, and they fed the people. After everyone was satisfied, the leftovers amounted to twelve basketfuls—about two weeks of food for each of the disciples. Those leftovers were their evidence of the abundance and sufficiency of God's grace.

The question we must all answer is this: Do we have enough confidence in God's power and the sufficiency of his grace to step out and respond to the needs of the world?

Jesus invites us to come and live in the overflow of his love. When we trust the sufficiency and dependability of his love we will be freed to pour it out into the lives of others. That's the flow of grace. Amy Carmichael wrote:

> Recently I was sent a picture of a jug into which water was being poured. The idea was that love, or whatever we need, is poured into us like that. I don't think it so at all. I think of the love of God as a great river, pouring through us as the waters pour through our ravine at flood time. Nothing can keep this love from pouring through us, except of course our own blocking of the river.

Do you sometimes feel that you have got to the end of your love for someone who refuses and repulses you? Such a thought is folly, for one cannot come to the end of what one has not got. We have no store of love at all. We are not jugs, we are riverbeds.[2]

Years have passed since that Sunday evening in front of the church. Since that time a lot of love has flowed through my heart by God's grace. It is softer now, more able to love, less judgmental, with a keener sense of the breathtaking value of the other. The adventure continues. I have a long way to go. I can't wait to see what is ahead. Jesus is there, still calling and inviting me to step deeper into the flow of his grace.

# —Making Love Real—

What kind of person do you want to be: a receptacle or a conduit?

Read Isaiah 58. In that chapter are two lists of needs to which God invites us to respond (vv. 6–7 and 10). As you talk with God today, ask him to give you a concern for one of these needs and to show you something you might do in response to the need that will make a difference. Sometimes world-changing vision begins with a simple dissatisfaction with the way things are and a desire to respond to a need that's right in front of you.

# 12

# The Transforming Power of Choosing to Love: Obedience

❧

A few years ago our two youngest children recorded their own Lego commercial. They got out the video camera and Carole's tripod and set up some additional lights. Carole is a photographer, so they know the importance of lighting. The product of their efforts is hilarious and amazingly good. I say this without bias.

However, after a couple of hours of hard work things began to deteriorate—with increasing disagreement, frustration, and loud arguments. Carole decided after several warnings that the best solution was to take away the video camera. Brendan was devastated. He could not understand the decision. Things were going so well. They had been so productive. It's only natural to run into a few problems. He attempted to argue with her for some time and realized she wasn't going to change her mind. It was time to see if he could wear me down.

He knew that I was going to stand my ground in support of his mother, but became quite impassioned when I did. At age seven he was an articulate and unabashed defender of his own rights. He decided to try a new angle. "You know, I hear a lot recently, about America being a free country. But I'm telling you, Daddy, it doesn't feel like the free country in this house right now." He stuck with this theme of America and personal freedom for some time. I didn't want to stop him. I appreciated his passion and the drama. I could hardly contain myself. With time he seemed to realize how ludicrous the argument had become. When he could no longer keep a straight face I began to laugh out loud along with him. (I'm a tremendous disciplinarian.)

The bottom line of Brendan's argument was quite simple: "If you love me, you will let me do what I want to do. I want whatever I think will make me happy and I want it now. That's how I define freedom." Reminds me of more than one conversation I've had with God. The truth of the matter is that love does set limits and boundaries; there is no freedom without responsibility. Love has never meant "never having to say you're sorry." In fact Jesus said over and over again that loving him means doing what he commands us to do.

# What about Obedience?

Jesus was concerned about our obedience. He said that our obedience was essential to the health and intimacy of our relationship with him. It is not a matter of earning salvation or gaining favor. Obedience and self-discipline alone can never erase our guilt, or merit God's grace, or cause us to become different people. But self-discipline has a role in spiritual training (1 Cor. 9:24–27), and our obedience is a necessary part of the process of transformation (Phil. 2:12). Jesus' concern for our obedience was about friendship and intimacy, about allowing him to do the work in our hearts he longs to do.

> Whoever has my commands and keeps them is the one who loves me. Anyone who loves me will be loved by my Father, and I too will love them and show myself to them. (John 14:21)

> Jesus replied, "Anyone who loves me will obey my teaching. My Father will love them, and we will come to them and make our home with them." (John 14:23)

> If you keep my commands, you will remain in my love, just as I have kept my Father's commands and remain in his love. I have told you this so that my joy may be in you and that your joy may be complete. (John 15:10–11)

Walking with Jesus is not about works, but about working out the grace that he has put in our hearts.

When we know we are loved, then joyful, heartfelt obedience becomes possible.

Jesus was concerned about people who obeyed God outwardly, but did it for the wrong reasons. He taught that authentic spirituality is something expressed toward God. *When you give, don't give in the way the Pharisees do in the temple in order to be noticed by people, but give in secret so that your reward can be from your Father in heaven. When you pray, don't go out to a public place and pray out loud flagging people's attention. When you fast don't go around moping and unshaven and looking dour so people think, what a godly person, he's fasting isn't he?* (See Matt. 6:1–18.) Jesus taught us that such obedience falls short.

On the other hand, Jesus enjoyed the actions of those who obeyed out of love and simple trust in God—obedience that was as a response to grace. The woman who washed Jesus' feet with her tears and hair loved greatly because her many sins were forgiven (Luke 7:38). The widow who gave two small copper coins expressed profound trust in God by her willingness to give all that she had out of her poverty (Luke 21:1–4). A Roman centurion expressed confidence in Jesus' ability to heal at a distance and was named a champion of faith (Luke 7:1–10). In each case, Jesus celebrated the condition of their hearts.

There is far more to loving Jesus than learning correct doctrine and the routines and rituals of the Christian life. If following Jesus is to be life-giving, liberating, and transforming, our obedience must flow from the deep understanding that we are loved. God wants to be more than a philosophical idea that knocks around in our head, and more than a master who receives sterile surrender of our will. He desires more than a rigid, legalistic resolve to play by the rules. Jesus wants our affection and adoration. He wants our hearts.

## Opening Up the Channels of His Grace

In the gospel of Luke, on three different occasions, Jesus was invited to the home of a Pharisee for a meal. In each encounter we learn something new about Jesus' concern for the condition of our hearts (Luke 7:36–50; 11:37–54; and 14:1–14). One of these encounters provides insight into the role of obedience in the transformation of our hearts:

> When Jesus had finished speaking, a Pharisee invited him to eat with him; so he went in and reclined at the table. But the Pharisee was surprised when he noticed that Jesus did not first wash before the meal.
>
> Then the Lord said to him, "Now then, you Pharisees clean the outside of the cup and dish, but inside you are full of greed and wickedness. You foolish people! Did not the one who made the outside make the inside also? But now as for what is inside you—be generous to the poor, and everything will be clean for you." (Luke 11:37–41)

I have to admit that the first few times I read the final

line of Jesus' response it fell a little flat for me. I felt like I had to be missing something. On the surface it sounds like an invitation to practice more good works, giving to the poor. How does a mere act of obedience remedy an inward problem involving the condition of our hearts? Over time the significance of his teaching has become clearer.

Imagine a dish in your home, a common mug. This is my life, the Pharisees' life, your life. From the outside it looks pretty good. Sometimes looking good seems good enough. As long as we choose the right words and behave well in strategic situations we think were doing okay. But after awhile it can all seem phony, inauthentic, empty. There's a reason for that. The dish has an inside that cannot be separated from the outside. We need our living to flow from our hearts.

The dish has a real problem. The inside of the dish is not clean. You look inside only to find that the last person to use it had hot chocolate and didn't bother washing it out. Jesus saw this as a good analogy of our problem. We may look okay on the outside, but inside is the residue of sin and selfishness. All is not well. How do we clean the inside of this dish?

Take your dirty mug to the sink. Think of the water coming from the tap as grace. Put a little water in the cup and pour it out. Do it again, and then again and again. The inside of the cup begins to change. After awhile the inside is as clean as the outside. That's the flow of grace, the principle discussed in the previous chapter.

Jesus gave this Pharisee a crucial piece of advice: Take your food, God's provision, the little bit of grace God has given you—and give it away to the poor. Pour it into the lives of others. You will find that God will replace that grace with more grace because you are making a choice to move toward life in the kingdom of God, learning to love God and your neighbor. Now take that fresh grace and pour it out again. Now do it again. The flow of God's grace through our hearts will change us. Our hearts will change. Our motives will change. The inside will become more important, and we will learn to love. You cannot love your neighbor and remain the same person. Part of the work that Jesus longs to do in our hearts is to open up every channel of grace blocked by the plaque of sin and self-orientation. He wants to do more than provide a bypass around the blockage. He wants to give us new hearts, working as they were created to work, loving God and loving other people.

## Understanding the Father's Heart

Jesus once told a story about two brothers. The brothers looked very different on the surface, but by the end of the story, we realize that the brothers had one crucial thing in common—neither of them understood their father.

The younger brother saw the father as a real kill-joy, so bound by duty and responsibility that he didn't know how to have a good time. He was backward, out of touch with life. Wanting to break free from his father's restrictive grasp, he demanded his part of the inheritance in advance. In that culture, such a demand would have been considered heartless and ruthless, an open rejection of the father. Even so, his father granted his request.

After squandering all of the money on drugs, alcohol, sex, and every attainable source of pleasure, the son found himself alone, living on the streets, impoverished, lonely, and miserable. Then he remembered his father. He knew his father to be good and kind and that his father would take him in again—not as a son, but as a servant. He didn't believe he could ever be a son again. He had messed things up too badly and he felt too much shame.

Upon his return home, he was shocked by his father's grace and forgiveness. He did not expect the love, joy, and celebration his father lavished upon him. He had no comprehension of the tender, loving, gracious heart that had always characterized his father.

The older brother, however, was enraged and hurt by the love and acceptance the father extended to his younger brother, whom he considered the ultimate messup. The older brother reminded himself that he never would have behaved so recklessly. He was dedicated and responsible and had always worked hard to please his father and gain his approval. He felt that his father had never shown him the kind of love he had extended to his sinful brother. His father had never done the kinds of things for him that in his eyes might have caused him to feel special. He, too, failed to understand his father's heart. He could not love his brother because he did not feel loved himself. The father tried to explain the depths of his care—that he had always been there for his son, that everything he had belonged to the son as well—but the older brother failed to grasp his father's love.

God has already decided what he feels about you. Apart from your obedience he loves you (John 3:16; Rom. 5:8). While you were a sinner, at odds with him and his enemy, Jesus Christ died for you. You can do nothing to make God love you more. Nothing you can do will make him love you less. He has amazingly gracious intentions concerning your life. If you're his child, all barriers have been torn down, and he is as close to you right now as he can possibly be. You cannot be any nearer to God than you already are. And if you are not his child, you are just one moment and one decision away from such a relationship.

## It's about Relationship

More than anything else, Christianity is about relationship with God. This is easily missed. In fact, the Christian experience is commonly explained like this:

Get Saved ⟶ Living the Christian Life

You become a Christian, and then begin doing things differently, according to a new set of principles and directives. But is this really what happens? Dallas Willard explained that "what sometimes goes on in all sorts of Christian institutions is not formation of people in the character of Christ; it's teaching of outward conformity.... It is important to understand that character formation is not behavior modification."[1]

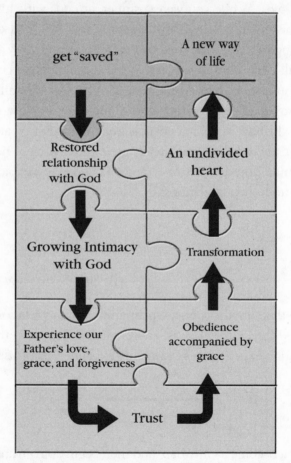

The problem with the "get saved, then change your

lifestyle" description of Christianity is that it completely ignores the essential centrality of *our life with Jesus*. We are involved in an ongoing, transforming relationship with God; *this* is where the learning and growing take place that lead to a new way of living. Without a relationship with God as the focus, Christianity becomes nothing more than a code of conduct, a system that tells us who's in and who's out. It has nothing to do with authentic transformation and change from the inside out. A fuller understanding of walking with Jesus might look something like this.

"Getting saved" and living differently are what happens above the line, the top two pieces of the puzzle. But what is really going on in the rest of the puzzle isn't always visible because it happens on the inside, in our hearts. When God gives us new life he restores us to relationship with himself—a growing and dynamic relationship intended to engage our whole being. As the relationship unfolds we begin to discover what he is really like, experiencing a level of commitment, grace, and kindness that exceeds any human relationship. Out of an awareness of his competence and dependability we discover a growing capacity for trust. Trust leads to faith, courage, and obedience—a desire to live in the kingdom of God and to make a difference in the world for God's glory. Obedience and cooperation with the Holy Spirit invite a deeper work of awakening and transformation. All of this produces a changed heart and a new way of seeing the world, resulting in a new way of living and loving.

# Obedience and Love

I think of my great-grandparents every day. They died when I was twelve about a year apart from each other. They were always bigger than life to me. In 1910, they married in the town where they grew up in southern Illinois. Soon after that they packed up everything they owned and along with their parents moved by horse-drawn wagon to the west, where they grubstaked a farm in southern Idaho.

My great-grandfather is a model to me of what it is to be a man. When I was with him I carefully studied his every word and movement. He taught me things like how to play chess and checkers, how to make and fly a kite, how to box, how to plant a garden, how to make a tomahawk from wood and stone. What I remember most was his character—his fairness, his kindness, his love. I cannot remember the sound of his voice, but I can clearly recall the way his words made me feel. I felt safe in his love. Sometimes we would build things together in his shop. Fond memories of working side by side with him have contributed in part to my enjoyment of woodworking as a hobby.

I have to admit, as much as I loved my great-grandfather, sometimes he would put me to work planting a garden or weeding, and my heart wasn't in it. I would get bored or tired and would want to do something else. I would see my brother and sister out playing in the street, riding their bikes. A lot of times

I didn't work with a willing spirit, or I would figure out a way to get out of work altogether and run off to play.

In my forties now, I've learned a lot about love, and I know a few things now I didn't know when I was ten. I know how much my great-grandfather meant to me, the depth of love I feel for him. I often think of how I would cherish a few hours in the woodshop with him. Once in a while over the years I have a dream in which I find one of my great-grandparents alive and I am overwhelmed with joy to the point of tears. I would give anything I own to spend a day on my hands and knees pulling weeds for the joy of seeing my great-grandfather's kind face, feeling the warmth of his love, simply being with him.

Richard Foster wrote, "Today the heart of God is an open wound of love. He aches over our distance and preoccupation. He mourns that we do not draw near to him. He grieves that we have forgotten him. He weeps over our obsession with muchness and manyness. He longs for our presence."[2] Do we understand how much God grieves over whatever causes us to hold him at a distance? (See Hos. 11:1–4; Matt. 23:37.)

# An Open Heart

Psalm 139 describes the pervasive and inescapable presence of God in our lives as well as the extensive, all-encompassing knowledge he has of each of us. God knows our thoughts before we speak them. He knows the story of our lives before we are conceived. It has always seemed a bit incongruous to me that David explained God's comprehensive knowledge of our lives so vividly yet concluded the psalm with this request: "Search me, God, and know my heart; test me and know my anxious thoughts."

What else is there for God to know?

In marriage there is a knowing deeper than the knowing in any other human relationship. But there are limits to that knowing. No other human can ever know everything about us. We don't even know ourselves well enough to share all there is to know. And there are different kinds of knowing. In any relationship there is what I would describe as *knowing as a fact* versus *being known because we choose to be known*—the kind of knowing that leads to intimacy.

If we're at a friend's for dinner and someone says something to Carole that hurts her, it is one thing to know her well enough to understand how she responds to certain words, to discern what her expressions mean, to know that she is hurt. That's one kind of knowing, knowing as a fact, and it's important. But, if on the way home, Carole shares with me that when someone said a particular thing she felt offended and wounded, a whole different kind of knowing becomes possible. She has opened up, invited me inside.

I think the same thing is true in our relationship with God. God knows us as a fact more extensively than we can imagine, but a different kind of knowing happens when we invite him to come and search our hearts.

Revelation 3:20 is often used to explain to people who haven't chosen to follow Jesus how they can invite him into their lives. But in this verse Jesus was talking to a local gathering of believers. "Here I am! I stand at the door and knock. If anyone hears my voice and opens the door, I will come in and eat with them, and they with me." It is possible to practice Christianity without Christ. But he is always knocking. He wants in. He wants our hearts.

## —Making Love Real—

Obedience is an expression of love in our relationship with God as well as a facilitator of love's growth. Love makes obedience a joy. When we love God passionately we will long to do his will. Obedience keeps us on the path of committed love. Obedience points our will in the direction of God's will, freeing him to do a deeper work of transformation in us.

Read Psalm 139:23–24. Personalize David's prayer and make it your prayer. Ask God to come and fill your heart with his presence and love you through the Holy Spirit. Ask him to lead you and to give you a passionate desire to obey out of your love for him.

# 13

# Loving Those Who Are Difficult to Love: Mercy

Our approach to justice even in our personal relationships involves the careful allocation of blame:

- We don't want to be misunderstood or to take responsibility for things we didn't do.
- If we can just decide who did what and who said what then we may be able to assign the larger percentage of the blame to the other person.
- We do not want to apologize for things when we do not see ourselves as wrong.
- Our system of justice is rooted in the idea of the necessity of establishing with evidence the guilt of an individual, and we carry this concept into our personal relationships.
- When we find examples of innocent people suffering for the guilty, such situations violate our sense of fairness.

We don't fully understand the message of Christianity until we feel it grate against our human sensibilities. The one innocent person, the only one who never did anything wrong, took upon himself the guilt of all the rest; as a result, the guilty pay nothing but freely receive grace, pardon, and forgiveness. "God made him who had no sin to be sin for us, so that in him we might become the righteousness of God" (2 Cor. 5:21).

Where is the justice in this? How can this be fair?

What we receive from God has no relationship to what we deserve. The quality of mercy extended to us by Jesus defies human explanation. "For the wages of sin is death, but the gift of God is eternal life in Christ Jesus our Lord" (Rom. 6:23).

Jesus told a story about a landowner who hired men to work for him beginning in the early morning and agreed upon a wage. He hired others throughout the day, even as late as five in the afternoon. At the end of the day those hired first had worked as much as ten hours longer than those hired last. The landowner paid all the workers the same wage, the amount he had promised to those he hired first. But those who had worked the longest were no longer satisfied with the wage to which they had agreed. At the end of the story the landowner proclaimed, "'Don't I have the right to do what I want with my own money? Or are you envious because I am generous?' So the last will be first, and the first will be last" (Matt. 20:15–16).

Jesus taught us that this is what the kingdom of

YOU WERE MADE FOR LOVE

heaven is like. God deeply loves runaways, adulterers, cheaters, and every other sort of offender—and desires a relationship with them enough to do the arduous and painful work of removing all obstacles to relationship. We don't have to see the justice in what God does, because he can do what he wants, just like the landowner. It leaves us scratching our heads, confused and perplexed by God's kind of generosity and kindness.

If we live with the good news long enough we can lose our sense of how radical it is, and even become bored with the message. Do we have a sustainable sense of awe and excitement over the nature of God's grace? Paul writes, "You see, at just the right time, when we were still powerless, Christ died for the ungodly. Very rarely will anyone die for a righteous person, though for a good person someone might possibly dare to die. *But God* demonstrates his own love for us in this: While we were still sinners, Christ died for us.... For if, while we were God's enemies, we were reconciled to him through the death of his Son, how much more, having been reconciled, shall we be saved through his life!" (Rom. 5:6–8, 10). Properly spoken, the words "But God ..." require rowdy exclamation. God's love is revolutionary. As Paul says, even if we can find examples of people laying down their lives for those they consider friends and moral equals, people faced with injustice who deserve help, this is rare. The idea of an innocent person suffering and dying for an offending party, the enemy, is gravel in the gears of our finely tuned sense of justice. God's behavior seems a bit quirky by human standards.

Who deserves God's grace? What did we do to prove ourselves worthy of his kindness? How did we merit his favor? What did we do to win his affection and mercy? There is nothing we could do to change our circumstances as enemies of God, "but because of his great love for us, God, who is rich in mercy, made us alive with Christ even when we were dead in transgressions—it is by grace you have been saved" (Eph. 2:4–5). God gives grace and mercy freely to undeserving people.

God is not obligated to be kind to us. The only thing he owes us is the justice and condemnation we incur by our own choices and actions. God does not set aside his justice in order to demonstrate his mercy. Nothing about the justice of God prevents him from expressing mercy. God is free to pour out his grace. "It does not, therefore, depend on human desire or effort, but on God's mercy" (Rom. 9:16). God's freedom to pour out his kindness and mercy is revealed in the cross. The just penalty for our sin fell upon Jesus as he died for us. If God's mercy is an expression of his goodness and kindness, which causes him to respond to human need, his grace is his delight in loving guilty, difficult, undeserving people and giving them eternal life and all the benefits of being his children.

Jesus recognized our capacity to receive grace and mercy from God and still hold to a system of assigning blame in our other relationships. He told the story of a man who owed a great debt of ten thousand bags of gold to a king. On threat of being sold as a slave along with his family the man begged for mercy and the king forgave his debt. This man went out and found another servant who owed him a relatively small debt of a hundred pieces of silver. He physically assaulted the man, threatened him, and had him thrown into prison. The king was so enraged by the behavior of the one who had received mercy that he handed him over to be tortured and imprisoned until his debt was paid. Jesus said that to fail to express the mercy shown to us by God in all of our relationships is the worst kind of folly (Matt. 18:21–35).

How important is it to God that we convey to others the mercy he shows us?

> For I desire mercy, not sacrifice, and acknowledgment of God rather than burnt offerings. (Hos. 6:6)

> He has shown all you people what is good. And what does the LORD require of you? To act justly and to love mercy and to walk humbly with your God. (Mic. 6:8)

> "Woe to you, teachers of the law and Pharisees, you hypocrites! You give a tenth of your spices—mint, dill, and cumin. But you have neglected the more important matters of the law—justice, mercy and faithfulness. You should have practiced the latter, without neglecting the former." (Matt. 23:23)

> Speak and act as those who are going to be judged by the law that gives freedom, because judgment without mercy will be shown to anyone who has not been merciful. Mercy triumphs over judgment. (James 2:12–13)

# The Radical Implications of God's Mercy

It's not enough to understand that God loves us, or how much he loves us. We also have to understand *how he loves us* if we hope to learn to love the way he does.

Paul admonished believers to always be "forgiving each other, just as in Christ God forgave you" (Eph. 4:32). Without a precise understanding of the nature of God's forgiveness, we may not understand how we are to forgive others. We may fail to realize that the high standard Jesus sets for loving others is not metaphorical.

The biographical movie *Gandhi* portrays an interesting exchange between Gandhi and a Protestant minister, Charlie Andrews, who came to join him in his work. As they are walking together they approach three menacing teenagers threatening violence. Charlie suggests a different route but Gandhi presses on, encouraging Charlie to stay with him. Gandhi reminds Charlie of Jesus' teaching regarding the need to respond to a blow from an enemy by turning the other cheek. As they get closer, the tension and sense of threat grow until Charlie expresses his fear and anxiety. "I think perhaps the phrase was used metaphorically." Gandhi calmly replies, "I am not so sure. I have thought about it a great deal, and I suspect he meant you must show courage, be willing to take a blow, several blows, to show you will not strike back, nor will you be turned aside. And when you do that, it calls on something in human nature, something that makes his hatred for you decrease and his respect increase. I think Christ grasped that, and I have seen it work."

Charlie speaks for many followers of Jesus who are confused by the high standards Christ sets for loving people. Charlie seems like a nice person, ordained after years of seminary and training. He has read the Bible and knows the words. But it is Gandhi, a Hindu, who endeavors to put them into action.

What are we going to do with the teachings of Jesus that call us to a higher way of living? It seems to me that until we allow the radical nature of God's grace to sink in and shake us up at our core, we are going to have a hard time taking his words seriously.

# Difficult People

We all have people in our lives who are "difficult." This is inevitable because every day we rub shoulders with people who are just like us—hurting, struggling, and broken. It's tempting to categorize and define the characteristics of people who wear us out. It's actually more complicated than that. When we think of difficult people, we need to remember that they may be a positive and energizing presence in the lives of other people. It's not just something about them that makes them difficult; a lot of the time it's also something about us. It's likely that every one of us is the "difficult person" in someone else's life.

It is easy for us to spot the error in our neighbor, but we tend to be slow to see it in ourselves. Jesus, warning us against the kind of judging that only God can do, instructed us to look inside ourselves first before we ever try to help our neighbors overcome their problems. "Why do you look at the speck of sawdust in someone else's eye and pay no attention to the plank in your own eye?" (Luke 6:41).

We can all think of people whom we encounter with dread, experience as emotionally draining, or who create in us feelings of discomfort and awkwardness. We usually make great effort to avoid them. But Jesus said that the way we treat difficult people reveals the condition of our hearts (Luke 6:27–36). One of the marks that distinguishes us as followers of Jesus is the way we love those we would not and could not love on our own.

Difficult people cause us to grow in ways we cannot grow on our own. Sometimes the person we find most difficult is the person we need the most. I know this statement may seem ridiculous, or a bit of optimistic drivel. But often, God actually intends to work for our good through people who may seem the most difficult for us to tolerate.

That is not to say that we should tolerate everything. Some people are truly difficult, and there are also evil people who do monstrous things. Jesus is not talking about tolerating abuse or evil, destructive behavior from others. He doesn't ask us to be door-mats. He does ask us to love the people who tend to make our lives difficult. But how do we do this?

C. S. Lewis, reflecting on what to do in a relation-ship with a difficult person, suggested that the best course is simply to do what you would do if you did feel love for that person. In other words, you choose, with God's help, to love them.[1] Dallas Willard describes cir-cumstances that confronted him with the choice to love or not to love:

> Some time ago I came to realize that I did not love the people next door. They were, by any standards, dangerous and unpleasant people—ex-bikers who made their living selling drugs.
>
> They had never tried to harm my family, but the con-stant traffic of people buying drugs, a number of whom sat in the yard while shooting up, began to wear down my patience. As I brooded over them one day, indulging my irritation, the Lord helped me see that I really had no love for them at all, that after "suffering" from them for several years I would be secretly happy if they died so that we could just be rid of them. I realized how little I truly cared for nearly all the people I dealt with through the day, even when on "religious business." I had to admit that I had never earnestly *sought* to be possessed by God's kind of love, to become more like Jesus. Now it was time to seek.[2]

Learning to love difficult people often begins with such a choice.

# Bearing with Each Other

Twice Paul used a phrase that can help us understand how to move toward loving difficult people. In Ephesians 4:2, he wrote: "Be completely humble and gentle; be patient, bearing with one another in love." And then in Colossians 3:13 we read: "Bear with each other and forgive one another if any of you has a grievance against someone. Forgive as the Lord forgave you."

"Bear with" literally means to "hold ourselves back, to restrain ourselves, to endure, tolerate, and look beyond differences in personality and opinion. "Difficult people can wear us down with their contrary opinions, unkind words, and hurtful actions. Like fingernails dragging across a chalkboard, they call out the worst in us, push us to impatience, and make us feel like we are losing our minds. Paul admonished us to endure and tolerate difficult people, but he qualified what he meant by including four different expressions of mercy—humility, gentleness, patience, and forgiveness.

We have already reflected on the importance of humility and gentleness. We'll look at the importance of forgiveness in the next chapter. Patience is particularly important to learning to respond to those who are difficult to love. The Greek word for patience is a picture of someone with a long fuse, meaning literally that it takes a long time before we get to the anger.

Does this mean we let difficult people run our lives? We need to set limits, to communicate clearly, to speak the truth in love, to communicate honestly about the way their behavior and words affect us. But patience involves another choice. Patience means that we refuse to let our irritated feelings erupt in words and actions damaging to the other person.

In medicine one of the foundational principles is simply, "Do no harm." In our relationships we may lack the skills we need to resolve conflict or communicate for intimacy. But sometimes the most important thing we can do for the people around us is simply to close our mouths. We need to make the choice in the moment, by God's grace, to do no harm.

Another expression of our impatience may be to simply push the difficult person out of our lives. Unless the person is your boss or a family member, you can get rid of just about all the difficult people in your life, have nothing to do with them, avoid them, dismiss them. But that's not really the answer, is it?

We all have friends we love who might be considered difficult. Perhaps some of these people have serious emotional problems. They may be disruptive to our lives at times. They call early in the morning to tell us things they don't need to tell us, and they show up at the oddest hours demanding a lot of time. They leave confusing and upsetting phone messages.

When we have relationships like this, there are always people who are ready to tell us what we want to hear, "You have every right to end the friendship. Just tell them you're done." But you know that's what everyone else in the life of the difficult person has done. Everybody's pushed this person away, without any explanation or compassion. Deep in your spirit, you know that's not the way.

We should be different because God didn't give up on us. When we were at our worst, God didn't send us away. He didn't say, "That's it. I'm done with you." He waited in patience. He is still there for us now.

I can introduce you to many people who will tell you how difficult I have been and can be. The people who have loved me most when I was at my worst have done more to change my heart than anyone else. They have taught me a lot about love. Their grace, generosity, and patience account for much of my understanding of love. They made God's mercy real for me, like a delicious, hot meal after days of fasting, hunger, and anticipation.

In the church today we have love, but it is usually conditional love. We like to think of it as unconditional love, but it is usually filled with conditions. When I was in high school I went to a church wearing the only pants I owned, a worn-out pair of Levi's with holes on both legs. An older man who was a leader in the church told me that I should come to church wearing my best clothes. I was too embarrassed to tell him they were my best.

The church where I teach and serve is the church where I met Jesus Christ and learned to walk with him. I first came here when I was five. The office where I work every day is the office where I knelt as a nine-year-old and gave my life to Jesus. Carole and I decided to worship here again when we left another church where I was pastor at the time I started medical school. Carole thought it would be a great place for her and the children. I deferred to her. One thing led to another. The pastor left. I tried to help out. People kept asking me to be the pastor. I kept saying no. One day someone I really respected asked me if Carole and I would pray about what God wanted. Up to this point, no one had asked me to pray. When we prayed my heart began to change. All I can say is that it's an interesting and exciting thing to find yourself a candidate to be the lead pastor in a church where a lot of people know every stupid thing you ever did. Gratefully, I have experienced years of overwhelming kindness, acceptance, and mercy.

## More Choices to Make

How do we get along with people who are different? How do we respond to classes of people our culture considers difficult to love? For example, how do we feel about people trapped in drug addiction or sexual addiction? How much room do we have in our hearts for the homeless? What about political and religious extremists? What about prostitutes or gang members? What about the sick? The old? The dying?

Part of learning to love means actively engaging those people we would rather close out of our lives.

These relationships provide tremendous opportunities for the growth of love.

Several years ago my parents divorced after thirty-eight years of marriage. My mother, who had always provided strength and stability for the family, came over to our home one day to tell me she was divorcing my father and as soon as the divorce was final planned to marry someone else. A few days later, without telling anyone, my father packed his car and moved to Washington, where my brother and sister and their families lived, to get away from the situation with my mother. I was devastated. I had just started medical school. Our third child, Brendan, had just been born. And my wife's parents were struggling for the survival of their marriage. I was thirty-seven years old.

You would have thought I was seven.

And I resisted all of this change. "What you're doing is wrong," I said to my mother. "I'm praying that you won't go through with this remarriage. I love you and that won't change, but I can't support what you're doing." A few days after the divorce was final, my mother remarried. I was not invited to the wedding; my mother assumed it would be too painful.

A man I didn't know at all was living in the house that I grew up in, watching the television set that I had bought for my parents, and sitting on my spot on the couch. Bitterness and resentment bubbled just below the surface.

Loving this guy was definitely not on my "to-do" list.

For two weeks I walked around in a state of emotional upheaval. I dealt with it the way I often deal with things—all or nothing. I wasn't going to deal with it at all, at least not right now.

Then one evening two weeks later, I abruptly decided to act: *I'm going over there, meet this guy, and I'm going to love and forgive.* Driving over there was the easy part. I slowed down in front of the house. It was as if the car would not cooperate. It kept rolling down the street. I drove around the block again and again. Finally I said to myself, "Phil, you're grown up; you're a big guy; you can deal with this."

I went up to the door and knocked, and a man that I didn't know from Adam answered the door of the house I had lived in almost half of my life. "Yes, can I help you?"

"I'm Margaret's son Philip."

"What in the world are you doing here?" His accent was thick Swiss.

"Well, I just wanted to meet you."

He invited me in. He asked me up front why I had been so upset with my mother's divorce and their marriage. I tried to explain. He was clear that he did not share my faith and values. The conversation was honest and direct.

I finally explained, "The reason I'm here is that I want to forgive you."

He immediately apologized with great sincerity, adding again, "I really don't understand what I did to hurt you."

That was enough for me. He clearly did not understand. We were both willing to move forward. I forgave. I don't know how or why in light of how much pain I felt, but I began to love him that moment. Forgiveness caused the walls to fall. With time, that love grew much deeper. I would often stop by the house for a brief visit and leave hours later feeling we had just begun to talk. I learned that there was a deep brokenness in his heart. Growing up in Switzerland, he had been sold to another farmer by his father when he was ten years old to pay a debt, and though his father lived another forty-five years, he would only see his father one more time in his life. He had never been able to forgive his father. When he was old enough to be emancipated, he immigrated to Denmark, then Canada, finally making his home in central California where he met his wife, Alice. They had raised three children together. Alice was killed in an accident at an intersection near their home, hit by a drunk driver, ten years earlier.

He treated me like a son. He became one of my best friends. God used me to lead him to faith in Christ and to help bring healing in his life. His love, concern, and support brought needed healing to my life.

Ueli died suddenly last October while he and my mother were visiting his hometown, Thun, Switzerland. The last thing he told my mother before he went to sleep the night he died was that he wanted to go home. He was tired and just wanted to go home. He had shared with me that he didn't know where home was anymore. He didn't want to go back up to northern California where his dairy farm had been. Monrovia, where he lived with my mother, wasn't really home. Switzerland no longer felt like home.

As I endeavored to comfort my mother and his family through the message at his memorial service, I shared with them the work God had done in both of our lives. Because of Jesus, Ueli had found a Father who never disappointed. He was finally home.

Here was a gift that we easily could have missed, a healing, life-giving love and friendship, love from beyond ourselves, love from the overflow of God's mercy.

Every day we are faced with the choice to love or not to love. What will we choose in our most difficult relationships? Will we give God room to work? It is time for us to seek to be possessed by God's kind of love, even for the people most difficult to love, even when we don't feel like loving.

## —Making Love Real—

Who do you find difficult to love? Spend some time with that question. Think about people of different ethnicities, people with different religions, people with particular lifestyles, people who sin in a particular way, religious conservatives, political liberals, people with whom you disagree, or people who lack particular social skills.

- Spend some time in self-evaluation. If not love, what are your feelings for these people? Why do you suppose you feel that way?
- Spend some time talking with God about these people. How does he feel about them? What would he want you to feel?
- Look for an opportunity to demonstrate love to someone you find difficult to love.

# 14

# Healing the Wounds That Hold Us Back:
## Forgiveness

Wₑ bring with us into every new day the memories and experiences of the past. For all of us there are parts of our story that are hard to forget: the injustices of life, experiences of being treated unfairly, the times when we were misunderstood, relationships that ended badly with no closure, hurts where no one ever said I'm sorry. How our past impacts our future is largely determined by the way we apply God's grace to our own hearts and the hearts of others.

## Forgiven

I am concerned that so many theologies today are driven by shame and guilt. Too much teaching and too many voices focus on the negative, telling us how bad we are. Paul tells us that *we are not who we were*, that in Christ we *are* new creations. The old way of life has gone and the new has come (2 Cor. 5:17). "For you were once darkness, but now you are light in the Lord. Live as children of light" (Eph. 5:8). You see, part of transformation involves accepting our identity in Christ, letting what God says shape what we believe about ourselves, and living out the truth of who we are.

Low self-esteem may seem like a psychological concept, but it has spiritual roots. It grows in large part out of self-condemnation. Even people who follow Jesus may continue to experience feelings of persistent guilt, shame, inferiority, and inadequacy.

For many years there was a wound in my soul that would not heal. It was a wound that involved the loss of a relationship. I had many wounds that seemed greater than this one—atrocious hurts inflicted by others that had healed long ago—but this one would not heal. Not too long ago I realized that the unhealed part of the wound had to do with my own self-condemnation. I had messed up and contributed substantially to the demise of the relationship, but I had not been able to forgive myself. The wounds involving the failures of others had been easier to heal. I could show grace to others. I had a difficult time showing grace to myself.

Along the way I must have assumed some things about God that were not true. I have to wonder, if we cannot forgive ourselves, have we really trusted in God's forgiveness of us? And if we don't trust in God's forgiveness, how can we believe when he says he wants an intimate relationship with us? Living with guilt causes us to be afraid of God and his punishment. As I began to focus on the reality of God's forgiveness and apply it to the wound, it began to heal. But I have learned an important lesson about the resistance of my own soul to God's grace.

## Forgiving

Forgiving others isn't easy. Jesus asks us to forgive the very people who have hurt us deeply and caused us misery. Forgiveness begins with God. We are called to forgive others the way God in Jesus Christ has forgiven us.

Without forgiveness we are left to an ever-escalating cycle of injury and hatred. Evil is like a piece of counterfeit currency passed around from person to person, because no one is willing to absorb the loss. Only Jesus, who never injured another, can step in and say, "I will take the loss. I will take upon myself all of the evil of humanity with all of its effects. I will bear it all and absorb the injury."[1]

Whether we are the offender or the offended party,

it is important that we recognize that Jesus places on us the responsibility to go directly to our brother or sister for the purpose of reconciliation. Jesus asks us to leave our offering at the altar in order to be reconciled first with a brother or sister we have offended before we offer our gift to God (Matt. 5:23–24). Jesus asks us to first go and privately reprove a brother or sister who has offended us with a view to winning them over before we do anything else (Matt. 18:15–17).

Forgiveness has two essential components—a choice and the follow-through. When we choose to forgive we let go of our hurt, anger, and desire for revenge and release the offender from the consequences of the way their actions affected us. Forgiveness is not denial of the pain and loss; it's not pretending that it never happened. It requires tremendous courage and honesty. It is a choice to see the offender apart from our pain and anger. We are freed to start over and risk further relationship.

Forgiveness requires follow-through on the initial choice, because sometimes we will be tempted to pick up the offense again. Forgiveness means choosing to live out in each moment and each encounter the grace of our initial choice. We persist in our refusal to let the relationship be defined by our pain.

Forgiveness is complicated by the question of how we approach future relationships with people who have wronged us. It's clear that we can forgive someone without their repentance or acknowledgment of wrongdoing, but reconciliation requires more confronting the offender with their actions; the acknowledgment of wrong and sorrow over the effects of their actions by the offender; the willingness to accept the loss, absorb the injustice, and choose to forgive by the offended party; and the mutual choice to move toward reconciliation. This is hard work.

Some may question the wisdom of forgiveness. As C. S. Lewis wrote, "Everyone says forgiveness is a lovely idea, until they have something to forgive."[2] I have heard people say that we should forgive only if the offender repents. Jesus does command us to forgive someone who repents (Luke 17:3–4), but he also asks us to forgive all the time, even in the absence of repentance (Mark 11:25; Luke 6:37; 11:4). Without their repentance Jesus forgave the people who participated in killing him (Luke 23:34). By clinging to unforgiveness, we commit ourselves to carrying the pain of the past into the future. We rob ourselves of the freedom God intends to give us.

Every month I receive a newsletter from my medical malpractice insurance company. Each letter begins with an article aimed at helping doctors understand ways to limit their liability. Two letters contained a two-part article on the power of a simple apology. The ability to admit we are wrong, seek forgiveness, and make a simple apology can be disarming and is a powerful way of facilitating healing in a strained relationship.

In the church where I first served as pastor, one of the elders, Tom, was a psychologist and a Native

American. He told me that over the years a lot of people have talked with him about the terrible injustices carried out against Native Americans. Generally people explain that these things occurred in the past and that they had nothing to do with it. Tom said that he never found such statements very helpful or satisfying. Once in a while someone would take responsibility, apologize, and even ask for forgiveness, expressing genuine sorrow for all the evil that had been done to Tom's people. He knew these people had nothing to do with the problems they were discussing, but he told me that he was always moved by their willingness to be wrong and that it helped bring healing to his heart.

Isn't that what Jesus has done for us? Paul said, "God made him who had no sin to be sin for us, so that in him we might become the righteousness of God" (2 Cor. 5:21). We spend time arguing and assigning blame while the only one who is always right and has never been wrong steps into the fray and allows himself to be made wrong so we can be right. Most of us demand a pretty high standard of proof before we'll accept we are wrong, while we label others as wrong with hardly a thought. The love and humility of Jesus invite us to allow ourselves to be made wrong more often for the sake of peace, healing, and reconciliation. This thought may cause many of us to bristle at the prospect of experiencing injustice or misunderstanding; but that is just another place where we have a lot to learn from Jesus.

# Today

We easily forget that life is a grace we receive one moment at a time. Paul said we are to forget what lies behind, and Jesus warned us not to worry about tomorrow. We are left with the present moment. The moment that just passed is gone forever. The moment to come may never be ours. God invites us to live for him now, to live fully in the present moment, recognizing that the kingdom of God is here and now. The writer of Hebrews quoted Psalm 95:7–8 three times, each time emphasizing the importance of today. "Today, if you hear his voice, do not harden your hearts" (Heb. 3:7–8, 15; 4:7).

A few years ago I received a long letter from a Cal Tech student who was part of our church. The letter detailed the impact my teaching was having on her life. She said that the things I said had sometimes proven more important than I probably realized. She originally sent the letter anonymously but later came and shared with me personally. Toward the end of the letter she wrote:

> This year you began a series of sermons on January 3rd regarding forgiveness. As I listened to these sermons, I asked myself whether I held a grudge towards anybody. And the answer always came back the same: my brother. He was always stubborn while we were growing up, and he would extort money from my mother by threatening me and others in my family. Sometimes he would threaten to kill himself if he didn't get his way. He lived in Asia. Last

year, I heard from one of my sisters that he had turned again to some old habits. As a result of this and other things I heard, I decided to stop talking to him ...

Over the last year he made several attempts to reach me, but I refused to take his call. My sisters would always ask me why I wouldn't talk to him, and I would say that I had nothing to say to him ...

One Sunday after your sermon you asked the church to write down the name of someone who had done something wrong to us, someone we needed to forgive. You said we should call or write that person that day. Later that day, I sat down with a pen and paper and I labored for a few minutes, maybe five, with the thought of writing my brother and decided against it. I didn't think it was that important. I told myself I didn't hate him. I was only sending him a message. I believe you made this statement on Sunday the 7th of February, when you preached on forgiveness. This date is important because if I had written this letter, it would have taken about two weeks to reach my brother. On Sunday, February 21st my brother died. He committed suicide.

This moment—right now—is all we've been given. Let's not waste it in unforgiveness.

# A Different Future

Emotional healing has come slowly but surely for me through a growing recognition of God's love. The forgiveness I've received and given has helped facilitate the emotional healing that has set me free not to repeat the past. As God gave Carole and me our children, I committed to the Lord that they would grow up in a very different environment than I had. This meant more than avoiding the negative things that can leave lasting wounds in our children, but finding ways to convey the high value I place on each of them and leaving positive memories of a father who loved God by honoring them.

One of the things that I have done periodically over the years is to recite to my children the stories of the days they were born. I describe the events with careful detail, explaining our emotions throughout the day, especially as they were born and we held them for the first time. We may be sitting at home or riding in the car and I will just launch into the story. This is one of my idiosyncrasies of which they have never tired. I love to watch their expressions as I tell their stories. Each of them has favorite parts that I must not exclude. Brendan loves the end of his story the best. As I arrive at that part of the story he gets a look of enthusiasm that says, "I love this part." The end of his story goes like this: It was almost midnight and I was about to leave the hospital and go home. I decided to go to the nursery to see you one more time. When I got there the nursery was full, but you were front and center and the nurse was taking care of you. A number of people were standing there and several commented on how cute you were. As I stood there I felt so much love and joy that I thought my chest was going to explode, and I pointed to you and I said, "That's my boy. That's my boy."

Years ago I read in Gordon Dalbey's excellent book on the healing of the masculine soul that the thing sons most need to hear from their fathers is not the words "I love you," but the words "You are my son. You belong to me."[3]

A couple of years ago, I took Brendan with me to visit someone in the hospital. As we walked holding hands, I said to Brendan, "I love you, buddy. You are so precious to me. I am so glad that you are my son." Brendan, who was about six, stopped dead in his tracks, looked up at me, and said, "I love it when you say that." Now I had made several statements and wanted to be clear about what he meant. So I asked, "When I say what?" to which he replied, "When you say what you just said; 'You are my son.'"

"See what great love the Father has lavished on us, that we should be called children of God!" (1 John 3:1).

## —Making Love Real—

Spend time today alone with God asking him to show you any areas of unforgiveness or bitterness in your life. Write them down. For each of these places consider the following steps.

- Invite Jesus into that place in your life and ask him to bring healing.

- If you need to forgive something or someone, make the choice today to forgive. If you need to convey that forgiveness to someone, initiate that communication today.
- If you experience ongoing guilt and shame over things you have done in the past, embrace God's forgiveness and grace now. Keep applying God's grace to that wound until it heals.
- If you need to make amends for wrongs you have done, begin doing those things now.
- If you remember someone who has something against you, go and begin to seek reconciliation now.

The goal here is to apply God's grace to our hearts and our relationships and to seek peace—peace in your relationships and peace within.

# 15

# A Life That Makes
# a Difference:
# Faith

❧

Love points us to the things that matter to God. Faith makes the choice to give our lives away for those things. If the love growing in our hearts is God's, it cannot turn a blind eye to the needs around us. As Paul wrote, "The only thing that counts is faith expressing itself through love" (Gal. 5:6). A life given to the things that matter to God is the ultimate adventure.

One of the most tragic yet subtle wastes of human life occurs when we choose to live for things that don't matter—even when living with great energy and commitment. It seems to me that things can only have ultimate meaning if there is a God. Otherwise things mean what we say they mean—which roughly translated means that everything is either equally meaningful or absolutely meaningless depending on who you ask. Without God we run a fairly high risk of believing meaningless things for meaningless reasons, resulting in meaningless living.

How do we decide what we care about? How do we determine what is important, what is worthy of our time, resources, and energy?

Jesus emphasized the importance of our presuppositions about the purpose and meaning of life. He told a story about a man who succeeded in everything he set out to do, but failed at life. He was a successful failure because he had inaccurate presuppositions about life's purpose. He built an agricultural empire. With the unusual blessing of true financial security set in place, he felt that he had fulfilled his life's purpose. But God called him a fool. (See Luke 12:13–21.)

Through the story, Jesus carefully targeted problems common to the human condition—self-absorption, materialism, the inability to recognize that life has limits. He challenges us to take a sober look at what really matters in life.

## Waking Up

I know from my own experience that sometimes it is not until I am slammed hard by reality that my eyes pop open wide enough to see what really matters.

While I was traveling in the Philippines, the axle of the bus I was on broke. For eight hours we sat stranded in a small village with one lone gas station. As I sat on a bench in front of the gas station, a young girl, about eight years old, barefoot and wearing a simple cotton dress, came up to us carrying a small basket containing about a dozen little packets of seeds. She was selling the seeds, which were for eating. They appeared to have been prepared by her family. I decided to buy a package out of curiosity and gave her the two quarters I had in my pocket. She looked at the quarters in her hand and quickly turned her back to me. I was confused by her manner and I leaned forward to study her face. She was crying. Big tears rolled from her eyes. I later learned that she was selling the seeds for an eighth of a cent per package. I had given her enough to pay for four hundred packets, more than she would probably sell in two or three months. What had meant almost nothing to me was very significant for her. I keep that packet of seeds in the drawer where I keep my watch so that I see it every day. It is a humbling reminder that I have little understanding of the vast needs of so many in this world.

Colin Morris, a Methodist missionary in Zambia, in his little book *Include Me Out!* described a set of circumstances that caused him to reassess his assumptions about what really matters:

> The other day a Zambian dropped dead not a hundred yards from my front door. The pathologist said he'd died of hunger. In his shrunken stomach were a few leaves and what appeared to be a ball of grass. And nothing else.

That same day saw the arrival of my *Methodist Recorder*, an issue whose columns were electric with indignation, consternation, fever, and fret at the postponement of the final Report of the Anglican-Methodist Unity Commission. Until that morning I had been enjoying the war that the issue had sparked off ...

It took an ugly little man with a shrunken belly, whose total possessions, according to the Police, were a pair of shorts, a ragged shirt, and an empty Biro pen, to show me that this whole Union affair is the great Non-Event of recent British Church history.[1]

We seem to be able to disengage the things we hold dearest on the inside—our deep spiritual urges and longings—from the daily life we pursue on the outside. Ambition, self-indulgence, and addiction numb our spiritual senses so much that "the deepest currents of our life no longer have any influence on the waves at the surface."[2] And we no longer hear God's still, small voice whispering to our hearts. In the midst of this haze come moments when we awaken briefly to what really matters in life, times when we see clearly what is truly important. Sadly, I often witness such awakenings in the final moments of life as patients face death and suddenly gain a keen sense of what is most important—often with feelings of profound regret.

Rabbi Harold Kushner, reflecting on the tragic events of September 11, 2001, wrote about those who realized that they might have only minutes to live. "Nobody called his office. Nobody called his broker. Everyone without exception called his or her family.

Almost universally, their last words were 'If I don't make it out of here alive, I just want you to know I love you and I love the kids.' The victims of September 11th, in the air and on the ground, included high-level business executives and minimum-wage kitchen workers, but in the searing crucible of impending death, they all realized what they might not have understood as clearly before: nothing matters more to us than our families and the people we love. Not our jobs, not our investments, not our plans for the future."[3]

How can we awaken *today* to what really matters? How can we gain perspective *now* about living well, living a life that matters, living so that we come to the end of our days on earth feeling that our lives have fulfilled their purpose?

# What Really Matters?

In Matthew 5, Jesus made a series of seemingly incongruous statements by which he stands the values of the world on their head. He began, "Blessed are the poor in spirit" (v. 3). Now what is so happy and blessed about poverty of spirit? "Blessed are those who mourn" (v. 4). What's so great about mourning?

And yet, each of these statements comes with a promise attached. The poor in spirit inherit the kingdom of God, those who mourn are comforted, the meek inherit the earth, the hungry and thirsty will be filled, the merciful are shown mercy, the pure in heart see God, the peacemakers are recognized as God's children, those persecuted because of their righteous lives inherit the kingdom of heaven.

I think that the Beatitudes, and perhaps the entire Sermon on the Mount, can be summarized in one simple statement. *Happy are those who prefer God above everything else, because in the end they are the only ones who are going to get what they want.* You can want whatever you want in life and if you're clever and work hard you can probably get it. But at the end of time there will only be one thing to be had—God himself. Jesus said that our hearts gravitate toward what we love and value, that our lives are shaped by what we care for most deeply (Matt. 6:21–24). Those who have spent their lives wanting God above all are going to experience infinite blessing and fulfillment. Those who have spent their lives wanting everything but God are headed for immeasurable disappointment and infinite misery. In the end, we will discover that sometimes the things we wanted most in life other than God are the very things that can destroy us.

We express what we really believe—our most serious convictions and deeply held beliefs—in the choices we make about how to live. We can talk all day about what we believe, but it is what we do, what we act upon, that tells the real story.

The human spirit operating intact instinctively senses what matters in life because we love God passionately and love other people. God's love worked out in our lives functions as a guidance system, a spiritual positioning system, directing us to the things that are of real importance.

I have sometimes speculated that if I did not believe in God I would be some kind of humanist. I have a passionate curiosity about people who haven't yet understood how wonderful Jesus is, and that curiosity leads me to some peculiar thoughts. I usually don't share these thoughts because a lot of my friends find it strange—and irritating—that I think about such things. For example, when I look at our human capacity for creativity and love, I am convinced that the alleviation of human suffering would provide some immediate sense of meaning for anyone, whether Christian or not. Again, I think there can be no ultimate meaning assigned to these things without God. But it turns out that this instinct to value another person just because he or she is a person, is not far from the truth.

When Jesus was challenged by a teacher of the law to explain which commandment was the greatest, he answered, "'Love the Lord your God with all your heart and with all your soul and with all your mind.' This is the first and greatest commandment. And the second is like it: 'Love your neighbor as yourself.' All the Law and the Prophets hang on these two commandments" (Matt. 22:34–40).

The primacy of love is reinforced by Jesus in the only new command he gave, a statement repeated over and over in the New Testament. "A new command I give you. Love one another. As I have loved you, so you must love one another" (John 13:34; 15:12, 17; 1 John 3:23; 4:21). What's new is not the commandment to love each other, but the way in which we are to love— as Jesus has loved us, with the depth of commitment and sacrifice he shows us.

The primary manifestation of our love for God is to love people the way he loves them. Loving others is not a separate issue from our love for God. One flows from the other. Mother Teresa had a simple message and theology: Love Jesus with your whole being and then love people as a reenactment of your love for him, one person at a time, one need at a time.

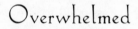

## Overwhelmed

We can easily be overwhelmed by even a superficial understanding of human need. Thirty minutes of CNN can make a person feel hopeless. It's easy to simply give up and feel that there is nothing we can do to make a difference.

Years ago I came across a story by a college professor. It was titled, "I Worried So Much about World Hunger Today, That I Went Home and Ate Five Cookies." In the story, Kenneth Lundberg described the frustration he felt about the littered stretch of grass between his office and the place he parked his car. It was always strewn with tennis ball containers, sweat socks, candy bar wrappers, beer bottles, pieces of cellophane wrappers, and other litter. Rather than complaining, he decided to take ownership, making a game of it and picking up ten items each way, taking them to his car or his office and throwing them away. Somewhere along the way someone in maintenance became a "silent co-conspirator" and placed large orange barrels at each end of the swath. "Finally, the great day arrived when I looked back on my twenty feet of lawn now perfectly clean." He continued:

> I've done this for several years now. Has general campus appearance changed? Not much! Have litterers stopped littering? No! Then if nothing has changed, why bother?
>
> Here lies the secret. Something has changed. My twenty-foot swath—and me! That five-minute walk is a high spot of the day. Instead of fussing and stewing and storing up negative thoughts, I begin and end my workday in a positive mood. My perspective is brighter. I can enjoy my immediate surroundings—and myself—as I pass through a very special time and space.[4]

We can live in such a way that God uses us to leave each "twenty-foot swath" we pass through better because we were there. And, if we do, we'll find ourselves changed in the process.

## Making a Difference

Scripture highlights three expressions of our love for God—prayer, obedience, and proclamation of the good news—as the means to radically confront the powers of death and accomplish things of eternal consequence. When Jesus proclaimed the Word of the kingdom, healed the diseased, delivered the demon-possessed, and raised the dead, he was manifesting God's kingdom in the present moment. And today, he invites us to push out the borders of that same kingdom through our radical participation with him in doing the will of God. These three expressions of love provide a way of actively bringing the kingdom of God into the present moment.

Jesus once told a parable about a persistent widow who continually bothered a godless judge until he gave her justice. Luke explained that Jesus told the disciples this parable "to show them that they should always pray and not give up" (Luke 18:1). After the parable, Jesus pointed out that God is committed to answering the cries of his people on issues of justice. "However, when the Son of Man comes, will he find faith on the earth?"—that is, will he find praying people, people who believe that God hears and answers prayer, that he can and will make a difference in the world? In the best discussion of intercessory prayer I have ever come across, David Wells describes prayer as rebellion against the status quo:

> What, then, is the nature of petitionary prayer? It is, in essence, rebellion—rebellion against the world in its fall-enness, the absolute and undying refusal to accept as normal what is pervasively abnormal. It is, in this its negative aspect, the refusal of every agenda, every scheme,

every interpretation that is at odds with the norm as originally established by God ... Or, to put it the other way
around, to come to an acceptance of life "as it is," to accept
it on its own terms—which means acknowledging the
inevitability of the way it works—is to surrender a
Christian view of God.[5]

The second way we can bring God's presence and
power to bear in the present moment is through acts of
obedience. Jesus taught us to pray, "Your kingdom
come, your will be done, on earth as it is in heaven."
When we do God's will here and now, the way it is
always being done in heaven, God's kingdom comes.
Through loving acts of obedience, we have an opportunity to provide a little bit of heaven for people right at
this very moment, right here on earth.

Michael was a two-year-old with Down Syndrome,
severely retarded, respirator-dependent, and hospital-
ized with a resistant pneumonia. His room was
strangely empty. No one came to visit. His mother was
in prison. He had no other family. He lived in a home
for respirator-dependent patients. Since Michael never
responded to those around him except to writhe and
make crying sounds, taking care of him could seem a
difficult and thankless job. While rotating at a pedi-
atric hospital I was assigned to his care.

I endeavored to spend as much of my free time with
Michael as I could. On a day when he seemed particularly inconsolable I stood at his bedside for quite some
time, determined just to be with him in his misery, talking gently, alternately stroking the top of his head then

his calf. After about forty minutes, though fully awake, he became very relaxed as if content. Since this had never occurred before, I was surprised. I found one of the nurses who cared for him frequently and asked her to wait with me while I attempted to show her what had happened. Sure enough, after thirty or forty minutes he relaxed, a level of response that none of the staff had ever experienced. We became teammates along with others in offering him a new level of care and attention. We strung some toys over his crib. We brought in a cassette player and began to play some pleasant music. More time was spent talking to him and soothing him. His second birthday had come and gone without fanfare weeks earlier. Though late, we planned a party and gathered in Michael's room with a cake, sang to him, and expressed our affection. I believe that the kingdom of God was brought into that room because a helpless child with no family was being allowed to experience the truth of about his life—that he has a Father who loves him more than you and I can possibly understand.

The third means of facilitating the growth of the kingdom is through the proclamation of the good news about Jesus. When out of love we share our understanding of Jesus and our experience of him—that we were wounded, broken, and spiritually dead because of choices we made to sin, completely unable to help ourselves, and that God came himself in Jesus Christ and paid a terrific price, dying for us, doing everything necessary to give us a new life and a new start—we give people an opportunity to hear, understand, and believe. God's grace works itself into people's hearts in a way that it can't if we remain silent. Paul said that he was not ashamed of this message because it is uniquely the message of power God uses to save human lives, that when people believe Jesus they step out of the kingdom of death and into the kingdom of life, becoming new creations—the old junk is replaced by something new (Rom. 1:16; 6:4; 2 Cor. 5:17).

Jesus invites us to join him in pushing out the borders of the kingdom of God, rejecting every agenda of this world in favor of his. We are members of a rebel band. From the moment we take our first step in following Jesus, we are out of step with the world. We are strangers and aliens looking for the way home. The road home is a narrower and less-traveled road—a road more difficult and dangerous than we first imagined—but as we travel we find tremendous joy, a greater joy in this life than those who believe they belong here and dig themselves in. If we refuse to succumb to the inevitability of things—recognizing that God and his world are at cross-purposes, but that God in his love will prevail—we can bring a piece of heaven to earth today.

# Love and Joy

It seems to me that happiness in life is a by-product of discovering what really matters and giving ourselves to those things, finding out what is important to God, what he feels deeply and passionately about, what makes his heart beat faster, and digging ourselves deeply into those things. When we understand the purpose of our lives and sense that our lives are serving that purpose the outcome is always joy.

Jesus has invited us to take up our cross and follow him into a life of meaningful and sacrificial service, but we cannot do what he asks unless we first make the decision to live as apprentices, following and learning, seeking to be possessed by his kind of love.

Will we follow Jesus into costly obedience and radical discipleship motivated by love? What will we do in response to the most pressing challenges of our day—poverty, hunger, HIV-AIDS, the misuse of sexuality, unwanted pregnancy, racism, substance abuse, violence, the trafficking of children? Can we join together without concern for who gets the credit and finish the job begun by twelve who turned the world upside down? Will we say, "Jesus, I'll do anything you want me to do with my life," offering ourselves to God in radical, world-changing commitment?

I believe that we can live lives of impact. If we make the choice to love passionately and deeply in our relationship with God and the people he has given us to serve, the flow of God's love and grace through our lives can rebuild cities, feed the hungry, clothe the naked, stem the tide of epidemics, build hospitals and centers of learning, reach the hidden people and everyone who needs to know Jesus, bring new life to the spiritually dead, see the Word of God translated into every language, and finish the work God has given us to do. As we learn to love as God loves, we learn to see with him to the ends of the earth and embrace the needs of the whole world with passionate concern and commitment. We find a way to serve and make a difference. It has happened before and it will happen again—among a Spirit-awakened people who make the choice to love as Jesus loves.

# —Making Love Real—

A life committed to loving with God's kind of love is the ultimate adventure in faith. You are an apprentice of Jesus, and he is here to lead you to go where he is going and to do what he is doing. Until we are convinced that God is kind, his intentions gracious, and that he is able to take care of us, moving down the road with Jesus toward greater love and sacrifice will be difficult. Ask God for the faith you need to follow him into a lifetime of obedience. Begin today to ask God to give you a vision, dreams of how he might use you along with other followers of Jesus to make a difference in the world. Refuse this world's agenda. You are a member of a rebel tribe. You are an alien and stranger here. Follow Jesus and learn from him to love as he loves. This is the path to the joyful and fulfilling life for which you were made.

# Benediction

May you know every day that you are deeply loved by your Father.

May you understand that the measure of your worth is what you are worth to him, and may you live in the confidence of knowing that before you existed as a single cell he already knew you and loved you and wrote a multivolume work about your life.

May you find the courage to face the depth of your need, to recognize the choices you have made to sin, and the damage that has been done to your own soul and all of your relationships. May God give you the strength to recognize and pursue your dependence on him, and the wisdom to seek the solitude where he will reveal the real condition of your heart.

May you be amazed by grace that exceeds all expectation. May you understand that while you were still a sinner, an enemy of God, God made the choice at tremendous cost to himself to send his Son. Jesus chose to empty himself, letting go of the privileges and honor of his deity, and came to serve you and to lay down his life, taking upon himself all of our sins. He did all of this because he loves you.

May your eyes be open to begin to grasp the breathtaking magnitude of his love.

May you live in the assurance that he loves you just as you are, but loves you too much to leave you just as you are. May you live in the joy of knowing that you are his precious child. You can add nothing to what Jesus has done for you. Let his grace release you from all guilt and shame. When you chose to follow him, he forgave your sin, ended the possibility that death gets the final word on your life, chose you as his apprentice, and walks with you every day to change your heart and to teach you to live in the kingdom of God.

May you learn to receive his love. The essence of your spiritual well-being is a growing love for God and people. Your capacity for love is a reflection of your openness to God's love. Open your heart to him. Let him love you deeply. Take his love into your heart and savor it every day.

As you open your heart to his love may you find healing and wholeness and may your hunger for God reveal itself as the true deepest hunger of your soul. May God himself come and satisfy that hunger. May you experience to your very core freedom from fear and the quiet confidence that comes with knowing you are loved.

God will never give up on you. He is committed to you with grace and mercy that will always exceed your ability to mess things up. As you experience his committed love, may you choose to stick with the people he has given you to love. May his humility in placing you above himself free you to honor others above yourself. May your spirit reflect his gentleness. May his love be made real to many through your kindness. May you choose to risk love.

As the Holy Spirit fills your life with an endless abundance of God's love may you choose to pour that love into the lives of others. May your life reflect the radical nature of his grace through the mercy, patience, and forgiveness you extend to others. May your life cause others to recognize how wonderful Jesus is. May your circle of inclusion continually grow.

As you grow in love for God and people may you experience an ever-increasing awareness of human need and the things that matter to God. May you find a way to serve, to invest your gifts, abilities, passions, time, and resources in building the kingdom of God, bringing his love to places where people live with darkness and suffering.

And may every day be filled with the joy of knowing that you are loved by the God of the universe, that you have his undivided attention. Amen.

# Readers' Guide

## For Personal Reflection or Group Study

The growth of love is a process, but it is a process with some clearly defined and necessary steps. The purpose of this book is to explore the strategy by which God makes us more loving people. These principles are organized around three basic questions.

- Where does love come from? Unless we know how to receive love from God his love cannot impact our hearts.

- What does love look like? If we don't understand the nature of his love we will not really know if his love is filling us and being expressed through us.

- How does love grow? We need to understand how God's love is worked out in all of our relationships.

The questions that follow are written for use by individuals or groups. I would encourage you find a quiet place, take your Bible and a journal, and spend some time alone with God, allowing him to speak to your heart.

# PART ONE:
# WHERE DOES LOVE COME FROM?
## 1 John 4:7–21

### 1. The Transforming Power of Being Loved: Significance

Key Principle: By understanding that our significance is based on the tremendous value God places on us, we are set free to love and serve.

1. Twice in Ephesians 1, Paul proclaimed that God chose us (v. 4, 11). In John 15:16, Jesus said, "You did not choose me, but I choose you …" Before you chose God he chose you. Why do you think this is important? What difference does it make?

2. Read Psalm 139:13–16 and Jeremiah 1:4–5. What do these passages say about the value God places upon your life?

3. What has God done to demonstrate to you that his love is real and trustworthy? (See John 3:16; Rom. 5:8; 1 John 3:16.)

4. Read Romans 8. Make your own list of all the ways God shows his love for you.

5. Read Ephesians 3:14–21. Write a prayer asking God to make his love real to your heart in the coming week.

### 2. The Depth of Human Need: Objectivity

Key Principle: For love to grow, we must understand who we are and what our problem is.

1. C. S. Lewis described "our whole being" as "one vast need." Why do you suppose he described us that way? What makes his claim true or false?

2. List all the different needs we have as human beings. Which needs are most important? How is it possible to have deep, important needs that we don't think about or feel much about?

3. This chapter makes the argument that it is important to understand our problem as humans in order to make sure the answers we seek are relevant. Do you agree or disagree? Why?

4. What did you learn about sin while reading this chapter? What makes sin a problem? Why do you suppose the Bible makes such a big deal out of sin?

5. How do sin and evil contribute to the problem of loneliness and isolation? How does the damage that sin does to our hearts impact our ability to love?

## 3. The Crucial Connection: Dependence

Key Principle: Living a life of dependence on God is essential to emotional and spiritual health.

1. What situations in your life seem beyond your control? What things about your life do you feel helpless to change? How do you feel about feeling helpless or unable to control things?

2. Read John 15:1–9. In verse 5 Jesus said, "apart from me you can do nothing." What does Jesus mean?

3. What are some things you can do daily to express your dependence on God?

4. In John 15:9 Jesus invites us to "remain in his love." How do we remain in his love? Be specific.

5. At the end of the chapter it is suggested that we have God's undivided attention every moment of every day. If you fully believed that, what difference would it actually make in your life?

## 4. Keeping First Things First: Longing

Key Principle: When our deepest longings are satisfied by God, our hearts are prepared to serve and to love.

1. Read Psalm 42:1–2 and Psalm 63:1–3. One of the main ideas in these psalms is that we have deep needs and longings that only God can fill. What do you believe about that? Have you ever experienced a hunger for God? How has that hunger expressed itself in your life? How is that hunger filled?

2. In the experience of the woman at the well in John 4, we see that when our deepest hunger is not filled by God we seek fulfillment in lots of other places—none of which ultimately satisfy. When have you experienced this kind of "appetite dysfunction"? How did you deal with it?

3. In John 4:32–34, Jesus said he had food to eat that the disciples knew nothing of. What did he mean? What was his food? Would our souls be satisfied by this food? Why or why not? How can we find this food?

4. C. S. Lewis said, "a man's spiritual health is exactly proportional to his love for God." Why is this true? On a scale of 1 to 10 (10 being "perfect"), how would you rate your own spiritual health these days? What caused you to score yourself the way you did?

## 5. Recognizing Love's Source: Openness

Key Principle: Our capacity to love is a reflection of our openness to the love of God.

1. Read 1 John 4:7–21. Verse 7 states that "love comes from God." In what way(s) does love come from God?

2. Read each of the following passages: Philippians 2:3–6; 2 Corinthians 8:9; Ephesians 4:32; and 1 John 3:16. In each

passage, God has already done what he asks us to do. Why is this significant? How do these passages deepen your understanding of what it means to obey God?

3. How can we open our hearts to God's love? How does opening our hearts to God's love impact our capacity to love?

4. Write a prayer asking God to help you open your heart to his love.

# PART TWO:
# WHAT DOES LOVE LOOK LIKE?
### 1 Corinthians 13:1–8; Romans 12:9–21

## 6. An Adequate Foundation: Commitment

Key Principle: Commitment, which is foundational to love, is a choice we make over and over again to act in the best interest of the beloved regardless of circumstances.

1. Read Psalm 103. List all of the ways God demonstrates his commitment to us. Read John 3:16; Mark 10:45; Matthew 26:36–46; and John 12:20–36. At what cost does God fulfill his commitment to us?

2. Why is commitment essential to love?

3. Read Romans 12. List all the different ways God has asked us to express commitment to people around us.

4. Dietrich Bonhoeffer wrote, "It is not your love that sustains marriage, but from now on, the marriage that sustains your love." What do you think this means? How does this principle apply to our other relationships? Write a letter to your spouse, family member, or dearest friend expressing your no-matter-what commitment to the person God has given you to love.

## 7. Making Others Important: Humility

Key Principle: Humility, which is essential to love, involves breaking through our self-absorption and choosing to honor others above ourselves.

1. Read Philippians 2:3–4; Romans 12:10; and 1 Corinthians 13:5. Why is putting the interests of others ahead of our own and honoring others above ourselves a necessary part of following Jesus?

2. What position, power, or authority do you have that you can leverage to serve other people?

3. Read Mark 10:45 and Philippians 2:1–8. How do you explain the humility of Jesus and his willingness to let go of position and power in order to serve?

4. C. S. Lewis wrote that the "burden of my neighbor's glory" is "a load so heavy that only humility can carry it, and the backs of the proud will be broken." What did he mean?

5. What do you think would happen in a group that decided to value relationship over personal gain and the need to have our own way?

## 8. Using Our Power for Others: Gentleness

Key Principle: Gentleness involves the choice to use our resources, influence, and power to lift others up rather than seek our own gain.

1. How would you define gentleness? Why is gentleness an important part of loving?

2. This chapter discusses the gentleness of God. How do you feel about the idea that God is gentle? How does believing in God's gentleness affect your sense of how he loves you and takes care of you?

3. Read Matthew 11:28–30. Why does Jesus tell us that he is "gentle and humble"? Why does he want us to know this about him?

4. How can you be more gentle in your relationships with other people?

## 9. Love Is Practical and Costly: Kindness

Key Principle: Kindness is the way we make love real to other people.

1. The main idea presented in this chapter is that kindness is the way we make love real to other people. How has the kindness of others accomplished this in your life?

2. Read Titus 3:3–8. How does God make his love real to us?

3. How do acts of kindness add credibility to our words?

4. In John 4:1–26 and 7:53–8:11, Jesus interacts with two spiritually needy people. What can we learn from Jesus about how to care for those who open their hearts to us?

5. What expressions of kindness can you give today to let people know you love them?

## 10. No Safe Investments: Trust

Key principle: There are no perfectly safe investments of love. We must make the choice to risk love.

1. What experiences of loss in your life make it difficult for you to trust in your relationship with God? With other people?

2. Why is trust necessary in our relationship with God? How does Jesus help us trust in the Father?

3. How does trust grow in our lives? How can we learn to trust if our capacity for trust has been damaged? Read 1 John

4:15–19. What can we learn from this passage that can help us recover our capacity for trust?

4. What problems emerge in our relationships when we find it difficult to trust?

5. Pray and invite God into the places of pain and brokenness that make it difficult for you to trust. Invite his help and healing.

# PART THREE: HOW DOES LOVE GROW?
### Isaiah 58:1–12

## 11. The Flow of Grace: Generosity

Key Principle: As we receive love from God and make the choice to pour it into others, we experience "the flow of grace" through our lives.

1. Read Mark 7:1–23. Why is Jesus concerned about the condition of our hearts?

2. Have you ever felt like attending church, reading the Bible, or doing the other things you do related to your faith are just going through the motions? Why do you suppose we feel that way at times? Reread Mark 7 and Isaiah 58 and look for connections between these passages and your experience.

3. Oswald Chambers wrote about "forming habits on the basis of the grace of God." What does he mean by that phrase? How do we go about it?

4. This chapter focuses on "the flow of grace." What is "the flow of grace"? How can we experience it in our lives?

5. Read the Parable of the Good Samaritan (Luke 10:25–37). What does this story teach you about loving? How do you

feel about loving people with tremendous needs—the terminally ill, the homeless, the lonely, those in convalescent hospitals, etc.? How can we grow in our capacity to respond in love to such needs?

## 12. The Transforming Power of Choosing to Love: Obedience

Key Principle: The flow of God's grace through our lives has a transforming effect.

1. This chapter suggests that not all obedience is the same. For you personally, what separates "good" obedience from "bad" obedience in your life?

2. Read Luke 15:11–32. This story is about two brothers. Which brother do you identify with more? Why do you suppose that is? What can you learn from this parable about your response to God's love?

3. Read Romans 5:8 and John 3:16. How does God feel about you right now?

4. Read Luke 11:37–41. Why is Jesus concerned about the inside of the dish? How can the inside become clean, according to Jesus? What does this mean for us?

5. Read Revelation 3:20 and Psalm 139:23–24. Write a prayer inviting God to fill your heart—every closet, every corner, every hiding place. Give him the whole of your life, all that you have, all that you are.

## 13. Loving Those Who Are Difficult to Love: Mercy

Key Principle: The real test of love is the way we respond to our "enemies" and those most difficult to love.

1. Think of the three or four people in your life most difficult to love. What makes them difficult to love?

2. Read Romans 5:6–8; Ephesians 2:2–5; and 2 Corinthians 5:21. What makes God's grace so radical? Read Romans 1:16. How excited are you about the message of good news that Jesus has entrusted to us? Why do you suppose that is?

3. Read Hosea 6:6; Micah 6:8; Matthew 23:23; and James 2:12–13. Why is it so important to God that we show mercy to others in the same way he has shown mercy to us?

4. What do we do with the teachings of Jesus that call us to a truly radical lifestyle of love? What will you do this week in response to his teachings?

5. Write a prayer today asking God to work out his love in you toward the difficult people in Question 1. Make the choice to love them today.

## 14. Healing the Wounds That Hold Us Back: Forgiveness

Key Principle: God's love and grace expressed in forgiveness lead to emotional healing.

1. Why forgive? What are the benefits of forgiveness? Why is forgiveness so hard for us?

2. What is the downside of unforgiveness? What happens inside you when you harbor bitterness and don't forgive?

3. Read 2 Corinthians 5:21. What can we learn from Jesus' example that may impact the way we relate to others?

4. Read 1 John 3:1–3. How do you feel about God calling you his child? Do you completely trust his fatherly love and care? Why or why not?

## 15. A Life That Makes a Difference: Faith

Key principle: God's love directs our hearts to pursue the things in life that really matter.

1. Read Luke 12:16–21. What can we learn from this parable about the importance of knowing life's purpose?

2. Have you ever had an experience that suddenly opened your eyes to the needs of other people? What happened? How did it change you?

3. How does a having a loving heart help us understand what really matters in life?

4. What do you believe is God's ultimate plan for humanity? How does your life fit into his plan?

5. Are you ready to follow Jesus into a life marked by love? Are you prepared for what such a life may cost? If your heart is ready, write a prayer offering your life to God for the purpose of radical, world-changing commitment and obedience.

# Notes

## 1. The Transforming Power of Being Loved: Significance

1. A. W. Tozer, *The Divine Conquest* (Harrisburg: Christian Publications, Inc., 1950), 23.

2. Brennan Manning, *Abba's Child: The Cry of the Heart for Intimate Belonging* (Colorado Springs: NavPress, 2002), 25.

3. Ernest Becker, *The Denial of Death* (New York: The Free Press, 1973), 3–4.

4. Ernest Becker, *Escape from Evil* (New York: The Free Press, 1975), 4.

5. Leo Tolstoy, *Confession*, trans. David Patterson (New York: W. W. Norton, 1983), 34–35.

6. Dallas Willard, *The Divine Conspiracy: Rediscovering Our Hidden Life in God* (San Francisco: HarperCollins, 1998), 15.

7. Anne Morrow Lindbergh, quoted in Alan Loy McGinnis, *The Friendship Factor* (Minneapolis: Augsburg, 1979), 101.

8. Brennan Manning, quoted in Philip Yancey, *What's So Amazing About Grace?* (Grand Rapids: Zondervan, 1997), 68–69.

## 2. The Depth of Human Need: Objectivity

1. C. S. Lewis, *The Four Loves* (New York: Harcourt, Brace, 1960), 3.

2. Paul Achtemeier, *Romans: Interpretation, a Bible Commentary for Teaching and Preaching* (Louisville, KY: John Knox Press, 1985), 66 (italics added).

3. Dietrich Bonhoeffer, *Life Together*, trans. John W. Doberstein (New York: Harper and Row, 1954), 107.

4. O. Hobart Mowrer, "Sin, the Lesser of Two Evils," *American Psychologist* XV (1960): 301–4, quoted in Paul C. Vitz, *Psychology As Religion: The Cult of Self-Worship* (Grand Rapids: W. B. Eerdmans, 1977), 93.

5. William James, *The Varieties of Religious Experience: A Study in Human Nature* (New York: Penguin Books, 1982), 140.

6. Ernest Becker, *Denial of Death*, ix.

7. George Wald, quoted in Philip Yancey, *Where Is God When It Hurts?* (Grand Rapids: Zondervan, 1977), 41.

## 3. The Crucial Connection: Dependence

1. O. Hallesby, *Prayer*, trans. Clarence J. Carlsen (Minneapolis: Augsburg, 1931), 17.

2. Dr. and Mrs. Howard Taylor, *J. Hudson Taylor: God's Man in China* (Chicago: Moody Press, 1965), 212.

3. V. Raymond Edman, *They Found the Secret* (Grand Rapids: Zondervan, 1984), 19.

4. Taylor, *J. Hudson Taylor*, 213–14.

5. Helen Keller, *The Story of My Life* (Mineola, NY: Dover, 1996), 20.

## 4. Keeping First Things First: Longing

1. C. S. Lewis, *Mere Christianity* (New York: MacMillan, 1952), 54.

2. John Piper, *A Hunger for God: Desiring God through Fasting and Prayer* (Wheaton, IL: Crossway Books, 1997), 14.

3. C. S. Lewis, *Letters of C. S. Lewis,* ed. W. H. Lewis (New York: Harcourt Brace Jovanovich, 1966), 248.

## 5. Recognizing Love's Source: Openness

1. Otto Weber, *Foundations of Dogmatics*, vol. 1, trans. Darrell L. Guder (Grand Rapids: W. B. Eerdmans, 1981), 407.

2. Lewis, *The Four Loves*, 126–27.

3. Ibid., 117.

## 6. An Adequate Foundation: Commitment

1. Ibid., 122.

2. See Helmut Thielicke, *The Waiting Father,* trans. John W. Doberstein (New York: Harper and Row, 1957), 17–29, for an outstanding exposition of this parable and theme.

3. M. Scott Peck, *The Different Drum: Community Making and Peace* (New York: Simon and Schuster, 1987), 90–92.

4. Dietrich Bonhoeffer, *Letters and Papers from Prison*, ed. Eberhard Bethge (New York: The Macmillan Company, 1971), 43 (emphasis added).

5. James Thurber, *Life Magazine*, March 14, 1960.

6. Paul C. Vitz, *Psychology As Religion: The Cult of Self-Worship* (Grand Rapids: W. B. Eerdmans, 1977), 9–10.

7. Ibid., 38.

## 7. Making Others Important: Humility

1. C. S. Lewis, *The Weight of Glory* (New York: HarperCollins Publishers, Inc., 1976), 45–46.

2. Henri J. M. Nouwen, *The Wounded Healer* (Garden City, NY: Image Books, 1979), 100.

## 8. Using Our Power for Others: Gentleness

1. Søren Kierkegaard, *Philosophical Fragments,* trans. David F. Swenson (Princeton, NJ: Princeton University Press, 1946), 25.

2. Richard J. Mouw, *Uncommon Decency: Christian Civility in an Uncivil World* (Downers Grove, IL: InterVarsity Press, 1992), 12.

## 9. Love Is Practical and Costly: Kindness

1. Torn from an edition of the *Monrovia Daily News Post* in the 1970s.

2. *Marty,* DVD, directed by Delbert Mann (1954; Century City, CA: Metro-Goldwyn-Mayer, 2001).

3. Lewis, *The Four Loves,* 42.

## 10. No Safe Investments: Trust

1. Erik Erikson, *Identity and the Life Cycle* (New York: W. W. Norton & Company, Inc., 1980), 57–67.

2. For a valuable resource on this subject see Robert Karen, *Becoming Attached* (New York: Time-Warner Books, 1994).

3. Augustine, *The Confessions,* trans. Maria Boulding, O.S.B. (Hyde Park: New City Press, 1997), 62–68.

4. Lewis, *The Four Loves,* 120.

5. Ibid., 121.

6. Evelyn Underhill, *The School of Charity: Meditations on the Christian Creed* (Harrisburg, PA: Morehouse Publishing, 1991), 55.

7. Immanuel Kant, *Groundwork of the Metaphysic of Morals*, trans. H. J. Paton (New York: Harper Torchbook, 1964), 63.

## 11. The Flow of Grace: Generosity

1. Oswald Chambers, *The Complete Works of Oswald Chambers* (Grand Rapids: Discovery House Printers, 2000), 1067. Taken from his lectures and originally published as *The Psychology of Redemption* in 1922.
2. Amy Carmichael, *Whispers of His Power* (Fort Washington, PA: CLC Publications, 1982), 235.

## 12. The Transforming Power of Choosing to Love: Obedience

1. Dallas Willard, "The Making of the Christian," *Christianity Today*, October 2005, 43.
2. Richard J. Foster, *Prayer: Finding the Heart's True Home* (San Francisco: Harper, 1992), 1.

## 13. Loving Those Who Are Difficult to Love: Mercy

1. Lewis, *Mere Christianity*, 116–17.
2. Dallas Willard, "Looking Like Jesus," *Christianity Today*, August 29, 1990 at www.dwillard.org/articles/artview.asp?artID=105, 1–2 (accessed September 12, 2006).

## 14. Healing the Wounds That Hold Us Back: Forgiveness

1. See G. B. Caird, *Principalities and Powers: A Study in Pauline Theology* (London: Oxford University Press, 1956), 98.

2. Lewis, *Mere Christianity*, 104.

3. Gordon Dalbey, *Healing the Masculine Soul* (Waco, TX: Word Books, 1988), 150.

## 15. A Life That Makes a Difference: Faith

1. Colin Morris, *Include Me Out!* (London: Epworth Press, 1968), 7–8.

2. Henri J. M. Nouwen, *The Life of the Beloved* (New York: Crossroad, 1992), 40.

3. Harold S. Kushner, *Living a Life That Matters* (New York: Alfred A. Knopf, 2001), 160.

4. Kenneth V. Lundberg, "I Worried So Much about World Hunger Today, That I Went Home and Ate Five Cookies," *His Magazine*, April 1984, 22–23.

5. David F. Wells, "Prayer: Rebelling Against the Status Quo," in *Perspectives on the World Christian Movement: A Reader*, ed. Ralph Winter et al. (Pasadena, CA: William Carey Library, 1981), 124–126. Adapted from "Prayer: Rebelling Against the Status Quo," *Christianity Today*, November 2, 1979.

# About the Author

Philip Carlson is senior pastor of Bethany Church in Sierra Madre, California. He is one of the founding partners of Sierra Spring Family Wellness Center, a family practice seeking to address the needs of the whole person, where he practices medicine part time. He is a graduate of Azusa Pacific University (BA, MA, Ethics), Fuller Theological Seminary (MDiv, ThM), and the University of Southern California School of Medicine (MD). He has extensive experience in teaching and training at college and graduate school levels and as a conference speaker, and has enjoyed a wide range of ministry experience in Asia and Mexico. He lives in Sierra Madre with his wife, Carole, and their four children. Last spring the Carlsons were blessed by the adoption of a newborn daughter, Ciara.